CONFESSIONS
OF A
COMPLETELY
(IN)SANE
MOTHER

CONFESSIONS OF A COMPLETELY (IN)SANE MOTHER

Kersten Campbell

Horizon
Springville. Utah

ISBN 13: 978-0-88290-849-6

Published by Horizon, an imprint of Cedar Fort, Inc.,
2373 W. 700 S., Springville, UT 84663
Distributed by Cedar Fort, Inc. www.cedarfort.com

LIBRARY OF CONGRESS CATALOGING-IN-PUBLICATION DATA
Campbell, Kersten, 1970-
    Confessions of a completely (in)sane mother / Kersten Campbell.
        p. cm.
    ISBN 978-0-88290-849-6 (acid-free paper)
    1. Mothers--Humor. 2. Mormon families--Humor. I. Title.
    PN6231.M68C36 2009
    818'.602--dc22
                                    2008045006

Cover design by Nicole Williams
Cover design © 2009 by Lyle Mortimer
Edited and typeset by Melissa Caldwell

Printed in the United States of America

10 9 8 7 6 5 4 3 2 1

Printed on acid-free paper

To my mother,
who taught me everything

CONTENTS

CONTENTS

INTRODUCTION

It is my desire that reading this book will inspire parents everywhere to laugh and enjoy their journey through the wonderful stages of family life. A sense of humor can help weather even the most stressful times within a family. I hope each person will walk away from this book with a sense that there are no "perfect" families, and that everyone struggles with the same issues, whether it shows outwardly or not. The Lord planned it that way. It is our imperfections that help us need each other and depend upon the Savior. When we "laugh often, love much," and rely upon the Savior to make up the difference, we allow ourselves to experience the joy that is available to all in this life.

The stories in this book are based on true events that have happened in my family, but I have seasoned each story with a generous helping of hyperbole for the sake of good storytelling and great fun.

The Campbell Family

Me: A tired mother who is not that talented at home-making, but tries hard to be extremely enthusiastic. I am constantly coming up with new and crazy ideas and taking them over the top.

My Husband: The straight man who is very stuck in his rut (except when it comes to sports when he just can't stop himself from letting loose). He is very practical, precise, scientific, and neat. He is the opposite of me in every single way.

Teenage Daughter: Serious, sometimes sulky and dramatic, and knows everything. Loves to lecture everyone. Highly intellectual.

Ten-year-old Son: The rascal of the family. Extremely curious personality, which leads him to try dangerous experiments. Loves to tease and is an extreme pack rat. He is always looking for ways to make a buck.

Eight-year-old Daughter: Doesn't really live in the real world. Extremely dreamy and loves to come up with ideas and invent "brilliant" things that leave us bewildered and speechless.

Four-year-old Daughter: Adorable and sweet on the outside, mischievous on the inside. Extremely happy, outgoing to a fault, says embarrassing things to people in the grocery store.

Two-year-old Son: Typical hilarious two-year-old behavior. Causes nuclear disasters all over the house.

1

rock and roll

You never know who is going to ring your doorbell. This time it was grade-school drug dealers . . . or so I thought as I heard my son answer the door and say to the two boys standing there, "Don't worry . . . I'll bring the money tomorrow. I've got it in my backpack. You just bring the stuff."

My son closed the door and came to the dinner table, while we all stared at him.

"Who was that?" I asked, envisioning what he might look like in a bright orange jumpsuit.

"Nobody," he said, digging into his spaghetti. "Just some neighbor kids."

"What did they want?"

"They wanted their money back."

"What do you mean, money?" I asked, thinking I might need a haircut for the newspaper photos of me sending my son off to jail. "Where did you get this money?"

My son shrugged. "Selling stuff."

I dropped my fork. "Selling? What were you selling?" I croaked.

My son continued to shovel spaghetti in his mouth. "Just rocks."

I stared at him. "Rocks?"

He grinned. "Yeah. Brian and I found some rocks by the side of the road. We're going to be rich!"

I took a drink of water. "Let me get this straight," I said. "You sold rocks to people?"

He nodded.

"And they bought them?"

He nodded again.

"What kind of a person would pay money for a rock?" I asked, shaking my head.

"Our neighbors."

I choked on a meatball. "Our *neighbors*? You sold rocks to our neighbors?"

He sighed. "Yeah. A lot of people weren't home. And some people told us 'Maybe later,' but a couple of people bought them."

I groaned. "Don't tell me you sold a rock to the sweet old lady down the street."

"What?" he asked, looking hurt. "They only bought the little ones. People said they couldn't afford the one that was thirty dollars."

"*Thirty dollars!*"

He smiled, getting excited. "Yeah, it's really big and pretty! Maybe you'd want to buy it!"

I stood up. "Son, you can *not* go around to people's doors selling them rocks."

"Why not?" he asked, genuinely puzzled.

"Because," I said, feeling hysterical. "It just isn't done! People don't want to buy rocks . . . they can get them out of their own driveways. You can't take people's hard-earned money and give them a rock."

My son looked crestfallen.

I sighed. "Okay, okay. Just go and give half of the money to your friends, and then come back and finish your dinner. And no more door-to-door rock sales, okay?"

My son popped up out of his chair. "Okay, Mom!" he yelled, as he dashed out the door.

Forty-five minutes later he hadn't returned. I turned to my daughter. "I thought I told you to get your brother from the neighbor's house five minutes ago."

She looked up from her magazine. "I did."

"Where is he?"

She closed her magazine. "I couldn't get him to come. He was too busy talking to people."

"What people?"

"The people walking by. You told him he couldn't go door to door, so he and Brian are wearing signs on their chests that say, 'Rocks for Sale,' and they are chasing the people that are walking by the house to the school musical."

I buried my head in my hands. My son, the entrepreneur. Anyone who could convince someone to buy a rock had a bright future in sales. Again, I had to ask myself: what kind of a person would buy a rock?

Later that night my son bounded into my room. "Hey, Mom, check out this pretty rock! Aren't the speckles cool? It looks like a dinosaur egg."

I picked up the rock. "Very pretty," I said.

He grinned, showing me his two crooked front teeth that hadn't grown in yet. "Wanna buy it?" he asked.

I looked at his smiling, freckled cheeks. "What would I do with a rock?" I asked.

"You could put it on your dresser as a decoration! See how pretty it looks?" His large brown eyes were shining and hopeful.

I sighed. "How much?"

"Three dollars."

"Three dollars!"

He looked thoughtful. "Okay. Since you're my mom, I'll let you have it for a dollar."

I always was a sucker for a bargain. Maybe I could pass it off as a fishing lure and give it to my husband for Christmas.

I looked at the shiny rock and remembered how my son's eyes had shone with excitement. I decided to keep it on my dresser, right next to the lopsided clay bowl he made me for my birthday. Eventually that beautiful boy would leave my home, and I would need something to remember him by. I guess *I* was the kind of person who would pay money for a rock. Especially when it came from a red-haired, freckled-faced, crooked-toothed boy, who had captured my heart.

2

booby-trapped!

"Aaaaaaaaah!" yells my husband as he loses his footing in the three inches of water that has accumulated on the floor after my daughter's shower. He bangs his head hard on the toilet.

"Grchgbtabobedkeakdlsseddghbo!!" he shrieks, holding his head in agony. This is a common phrase of his. He utters it each time he has been accosted by the thousands of booby traps left by his wife and kids over many years of family living.

It started out innocently enough. When we were first married, my husband noticed that along with my talent for cooking fish sticks, I happened to have a talent for stacking things . . . dishes, books, and freezer paraphernalia. My motto: if the pile is not as high as Mount St. Helen's, it does not have enough stuff in it. This great talent is how I have avoided putting things in their right places for fourteen years.

Can I help it if he happens to open the freezer every time I have stuffed an ice cube tray full of water precariously on top of a ham?

He was the one who opened the cupboard when all the spices fell out and broke a plate into his pancake batter.

And how was I supposed to know that shoe I wedged onto the top shelf of his closet would give him a black-eye when he opened the door?

Although these incidents live in infamy in my husband's mind, I am not the main trap-setter in my house. My kids are much more talented at it than I, and they target each other, as well as my husband. That is why yesterday at 10 AM I found myself vacuuming my toddler's forehead. His four-year-old sister had opened the powdered milk and left it within his reach—a disaster waiting to happen.

"Mommy, I make a mess," I heard him say, as I was holding my nose and gathering crusty socks from my son's bedroom.

Previous experience has taught me to drop everything and run when I hear these words.

By the time I got to my son, all I could see was a fluffy, white mushroom cloud where the kitchen used to be, two eyeballs, and a set of teeth, grinning at me through the haze.

My four-year-old is famous for causing these types

of nuclear disasters. She even booby-trapped herself one day.

"Mommy?" I heard her say, as I was trying to pick up the toys in the living room.

"What?" I said, trying to finish the job before my husband came home.

"Mommy . . ."

"Just a minute," I said. "Mommy's coming." I continued to pick up the toys.

"Mommy, I'm stuck," my daughter said in a calm voice.

"Okay, just a few more toys and I'll be right there. Can you wait a minute?"

"Mommy, I'm flying."

That got my attention. I stood up and wandered to where she was in the kitchen, dropping the rubber ball I held in my hands when I found her.

She had been trying to get into the chocolate chips while I wasn't looking, and while she stood on the counter, the cupboard door had swung open and knocked her off of the countertop. The knob on the cupboard door had scooped her up by the strap of her overalls and hung her up in midair, her legs and arms flailing helplessly as she tried in vain to get back to safety. There she hung, caught in a trap of her own design. I briefly considered leaving her there; things would be so much safer around our house.

But these are not the most famous booby traps in our

4

alice in mormonland

When I joined the Church twenty years ago, I knew I had found the truth. Finally, I had found a place where I could feel at home, a place of acceptance and peace, where people loved each other and shared the same values. Everywhere I looked, families were living eternal principles, such as the one that changed my life forever—"Mormon Standard Time."

I'm not sure what happened. Before I was baptized I hated to be late. I planned my life around appointments, arriving fifteen minutes early just so I could sit in the car in front of someone's house and pretend not to see the people staring out their windows at me, wondering if I was a stalker.

But as soon as I became a Mormon I experienced a mighty change of heart. This change miraculously allowed me to arrive at church fifteen minutes late and still feel like I was on time. My family's motto: "If you can beat the last verse of the opening hymn and get a

family. That award goes to my nephew, who whispered loudly to his friend in the kitchen, while his mother was nursing, "They'll *never* get past this JELL-O trap!"

He and a friend had made a red and blue Jell-O lake on the floor that was sure to trip up an annoying older brother or two.

You can't blame the kids. It's in their genes. They inherited it from an uncle, who decided one night to set up an elaborate burglar trap in his bedroom with laundry baskets and a ball of string.

This magnificently engineered contraption got its first test that night when one of the kids got sick and his father came running.

"Grchgbtabobedkeakdlsseddghbo!!" he shrieked, as he flew through the air.

So that's where my husband learned that phrase. I guess it comes in really handy. I think I'll use it the next time I fall into the toilet at 3 AM after getting caught in my son's "leave the toilet seat up and listen for the screams" booby trap.

I'll get him back though. Just wait until he opens his closet door.

3

zen and the art of zucchini

Ooooooh, what do you do in the summertime,
*   with all your squash so green?*
Do you take them downtown,
Wait till no one's around,
And stuff them in cars you walk byyyyyy?
Is that what you do?
So do I.

Aaah, zucchini. Also known as summer squash, scientifically referred to as "curbita pepo," with the baseball bat variety sometimes being classified as "alienatus your neighborus."

I believe that the Lord is trying to teach us important lessons through this vegetable. If everyone would observe the life lessons learned through the trials of growing zucchini, this world would be a much safer, kinder place to live. My children and I learned some of

these life-changing lessons this summer when for some insane reason I decided to plant three hills of these devilish plants.

Day 1—Me: "Kids, kids, look. We've got a little zucchini. Isn't it adorable? Hey, honey, come outside and look at this little thing. Could you bring your camera? I want a picture of the first squash that we grew together as a family."

Day 5—Husband: "Darling, I'd never criticize your cooking, but if I have to eat one more bite of "Zucchini Delight" I am going to move this family to Iceland, where they've never even heard of summer, let alone summer squash."

Day 16—Daughter, slamming the door and running into the kitchen: "Hey, Mom, I just saw the old lady next door and she said if we put any more zucchini on her doorstep in the dead of night, she's calling the police."

Phooey. What was a latter-day gardener to do? I was trying to live the commandment to grow a garden, but was I not also commanded to love my neighbor as myself? The trouble was, my neighbor did not love zucchini as much as myself.

I decided to come up with a plan of how to live both laws. Gleaning inspiration from a popular piece of fiction which shall go unnamed, I decided to become the "Zucchini Bandit," robbing from the zucchini rich

soft seat, you're doing great." This usually works because it is everybody else's motto too.

Here is a typical Sunday morning in the Campbell household:

Children, jumping on the bed: "Mom, Mom, Mom, Mom, Mom, Mom. Aren't you going to get up? Church starts in ten minutes."

Me: "Drat. I forgot to set the alarm again. Okay everybody! Find some church clothes and pile in the car as fast as you can . . . hurry or we'll be in the hard seats."

The children all rise up and wail in one voice: "Nooooooooooo, not the hard seats!"

We all scramble around like mad. Clothes fly out of drawers and panic ensues as we realize that the church clothes have been "misplaced." (Hey . . . I never learned that "Saturday is a Special Day" until I was an adult. I'm still getting used to the idea.)

My son shows up to the car in jeans and a t-shirt. "Mom, I can't find my white shirt. What should I do?"

Hmmm. I use my quick wits and tell him to throw his suit coat on over his t-shirt. "Maybe no one will notice if you slouch a lot in primary."

Teenage daughter: "Mom, why is the baby wearing plaid and stripes together? He looks like he's from the seventies."

Me: "Here, throw these flip flops on his feet. He's being 'progressive' in the fashion department today."

Toddler: "Mooooom, I'm hungry. I didn't get any breakfast."

Son: "Too bad we ate all of the cheerios for dinner last night."

I run back to the kitchen, searching in vain for any kind of church snack. In desperation I grab a loaf of bread.

Teenage daughter: "I am NOT going to be seen with you carrying an entire loaf of bread into church."

I giggle nervously. "Don't worry. We'll try and pretend we brought it for the sacrament."

We stumble into church just after the announcements. People give me sympathetic smiles as I slide into the front row with my five kids and no husband. I surreptitiously start to pass out pieces of bread, feeding my kids breakfast during the opening hymn, until I notice the sweet grandmother sitting next to me. Her lips are pursed and eyes wide with shock.

I lean over and whisper: "You don't happen to have any grape jelly in your purse, do you?"

She scoots farther away from me.

Well, at least I am doing some good in the world. I make all the moms who feed their kids breakfast feel really great about themselves. Now, if I can only think of how a loaf of bread ties into the primary lesson I was supposed to prepare last night. At least I have a nice soft seat to sit in while I contemplate. I love living in Zion, don't you?

5

family scriptures: aaah, the memories

I will always treasure the memory of family scripture study . . . where the whole family gets together each night to ponder in their hearts the bread of life . . . when the words of prophets and apostles elevate our minds and our hearts to unity and love, one to another. As we gather together in that beautiful family circle, I can see the impressionable minds of my precious little ones begin to mull over weighty issues such as how to pinch your sister without your parents catching you, or better yet, how to insult each other in Chinese.

These things may seem mutually exclusive, but they are really interdependent. For instance, if my teenage daughter hadn't interrupted my husband's first paragraph with a blood-curdling scream, we never would have seen my son's tongue sticking out at her, inspiring a beautiful oration from my husband on the perils of sin and death-bed repentance. It was too bad that halfway through the second sentence he had to stop when our two-year-old knocked him unconscious by whacking him on the back of the head with a brush while he was trying to fix his father's hair into a more fashionable "do."

The resulting scream from me, and the comical new hairdo on my husband, led each of our five children to fall to the floor in fits of laughter, losing their place in the scriptures when the book went flying through the air, hitting our four-year-old daughter on the head and starting her in a wail that would shake the foundations of the earth.

"Cwiptures!" squealed my toddler, grabbing the book and running out of the room.

"Wait! Come back here with those!" I yelled, panicking because this was the only set of scriptures that we hadn't left at church, spilled juice upon, or accidentally run over with the car.

"No . . . you cannot trap him under that thing!" I yelled at my ten-year-old, who began chasing his brother with a clothes hamper.

"Be careful!" I screeched at my eight-year-old who tried to tackle my toddler with a flying leap off of the couch.

Catching the boy proved to be easy compared to the amount of bribing required to retrieve the stolen goods.

Two suckers and five gummy worms later we were all sitting down, ready to hear the first sentence in the

Book of Mormon. It was the one we knew best, having never been able to progress much further than that in our previous twelve years of family scripture study.

"I Nephi, having been born of saintly parents . . ."

"Hey, that's not what it's supposed to say!" yelled my daughter.

My son, showing what he had learned from years of scripture exploration with his fine parents, flicked her on the forehead.

See? I told you their minds were being "impressioned." I love family scripture study. I just hope we'll be able to afford the emergency room visit afterward.

6

quick trick kid stack

"Shoot us, just shoot us now!" I yelled desperately, as I tried to gather my children into my arms. Panic seized my stomach as I noticed my two-year-old wiggling violently out of my husband's death grip.

"No!" I thought. "We can't let him get away." I closed my eyes, wishing they would just put us out of our misery. I couldn't take this pressure much longer.

It was a family photo shoot, and this was the seventeenth time we had tried to get a shot of our children sitting on the slide. My toddler started to wail.

The photographer, an unlucky neighbor who happened to be walking by when we had the camera out, spoke patiently to one of the children. "Now this time, don't stick your tongue out at your brother." Then she turned to me. "Do you think you might find a way to keep this little one's finger out of his nose?"

I chuckled, as if I thought this was a great joke.

My toddler, his wailing halted temporarily with a blue sucker, promptly stuck his finger into his father's nose, saying loudly, "There's a bug in there, Daddy."

"Disgusting!" yelled my other children, scattering in four different directions. For the thousandth time since having children, I wished for a bullhorn.

I turned to the next best thing: my husband. He let out a shrill whistle, and all the children came screeching back, trying to morph into the impossible pose we were trying to achieve.

I had seen it in a magazine.

"That family makes it look easy," I had complained, pointing to the picture in the publication after our fourteenth try.

"That's because they only have two kids, and they are professionals," my husband had hissed without moving his lips. He was trying to maintain his smile through gritted teeth.

The children all clamored around the family swing set once again.

"Quit pushing me."

"I'm not pushing you. You stepped on my foot."

"I was here first."

"Now children, calm down," I soothed. "Let's try putting the baby at the bottom of the slide this time."

We piled the children up the slide, one by one, like

stacking blocks, until there was only my oldest daughter left.

Immediately I saw the flaw in my design. Ever the optimist, I said to my eldest, "We'll hold you up, so try not to put any weight on the top of the stack."

She climbed to the top of the slide and looped her arms through ours. My husband and I groaned as we tried to defy the laws of gravity. Man, she had grown some in the last few years.

Sweat began to trickle down my spine as we tried to keep her from toppling the precarious "kid tower" we had constructed.

The photographer began to fiddle with the camera. "Everybody smile," she directed, crouching and aiming. Then she stood up, looking harassed.

"Can't . . . hold . . . on . . . much . . . longer," grunted my husband.

"You there," our neighbor pointed at our daughter, "what are you doing? Stop sniffing your brother."

"I can't help it," said my eight-year-old. "He smells like a camel."

The children all let out loud guffaws, and the photographer rushed to snap the picture while they were all smiling at once.

Unfortunately, the laughter made my daughter's head tip back, upsetting the precarious balance of the kid stack, and she began to shoot down the slide, taking out all the children in front of her, and bringing her parents down with her until we all ended up in a heap at the bottom of the slide.

Our neighbor finally cracked and ran away screaming.

I picked up the camera and examined the digital picture of our family heap. Hmmm. Not bad. At least she got my good side. Too bad my husband had landed upside down. I squinted. And there was the unfortunate fact that the baby's sucker had ended up sticking out of my oldest daughter's nose. Ah, well. At least it showed what life in a family of seven is really like.

All in all I'd say we were a success. The incredible tangle of arms and legs we'd captured was so amazing, I was sure they'd want to put it in a magazine. If you see us in *your* next publication, just remember, don't try this at home. Making a fool out of yourself is much harder than it looks. Just ask us. We're professionals!

7

the secret life of wives

Danger lies hidden in every seemingly solid marital relationship. Watch out! Disaster may be lurking just around the corner. You never know when it's about to strike!

The relationship trouble usually hits when the husband leaves town for more than a week at a time. The wife looks around at the unpainted stairwell, sighs over the cracked cement, and lingers longingly over pictures in magazines: pictures of what could have been. The pictures inspire a seed of desire that grows secretly in her heart until the husband comes home, utterly unaware, and totally shocked to find out that while he was gone, his wife has found a new persona . . . one he has never seen before. She has become . . . handy.

My own husband found this out when he came home from work one day to find me drilling holes in all of the window frames of our house.

"What in heaven's name is going on around here?" he asked, dropping his newspaper when he saw the maniacal gleam in my eye.

"Honey!" I said with excitement, my cheeks flushed. "I never knew how fun this 'thingy' could be. You can make a hole in just about anything, except bricks . . . I tried it and broke one of your bits, sorry."

"Thingy?" he replied, his face turning white. "That is a very expensive automatic drill. What are you doing drilling holes in all of our wood?"

"I'm fixing up the house!" I replied, laughing. "I saw a picture of some shelves in a magazine, and suddenly I realized, 'I can do that!' "

I paused, waiting for a reaction. Seeing nothing but closed eyelids and deep breathing, I continued, "In other words, great news! You don't have to do 'fix-it' jobs *ever* again! I can do them myself. In fact, I am going to remodel our whole kitchen!"

"Remodel our kitchen?" my husband screeched. He stopped and took a few deep breaths, trying to calm himself down. Then he put a gentle hand on my arm.

"Darling," he said. "Do you know what is involved in remodeling a kitchen? The cost alone!"

"Cost, schmost!" said I, waving the drill in the air. My husband jumped away when I accidentally pushed the trigger in his face. "We are going to do all of the work ourselves, so it won't cost much at all!"

His eyes narrowed, "What do you mean 'we'?"

I sighed. "Don't get all testy . . . I'll do most of the work, but you can carry the heavy stuff. You'll be the grunt laborer."

He grunted. "Gee, thanks. But, hon! Honestly people train for years, they have to become apprentices to learn how to do all that stuff."

"Not me!" I say, sticking the drill proudly in the holster of my tool belt. "Check out our bedroom window."

Again, the color drained from his face. He walked slowly to our room, like a man assigned to the gallows. Then he stopped and stared silently at the huge lumps behind the closed curtains, his jaw dropping, when I opened them up with a flourish.

He coughed. "Our window? You put shelves in our window?"

"Yep! I did all eight of them while the baby was sleeping."

He gulped. "But why? Eight shelves in one window? Why would you do such a thing?"

"Tomatoes."

My husband gave me a blank stare.

I sighed. "You know. I want to grow tomatoes from seed. We didn't have enough space in our window for the pots."

"But," he sputtered, "we can't even sit up in our bed without hitting our heads . . . how are we going to—"

"No worries!" I said, lifting the drill out of its holster and revving it a few times. "I noticed you had a saw thingamajig in your tool box! The legs to the bed are my next project."

I squinted at him, "Honey are you okay? Your face looks a little purple."

"I'm fine," he said, holding a fist to his chest. His voice sounded strangled.

"Good. Because I want to show you how I fixed the broken crib. You know what they always say . . ."

"No, I don't," said my husband, rubbing a wrinkle in his forehead.

"With a little know-how and a lot of duct tape—" I grinned. "Nothing's impossible!"

That's when my husband fainted. And so, husbands beware. Don't let this happen to you. Get all those "honey-do" lists done before you leave town. And *never* leave a home repair manual lying around where just anybody can read it. Especially if it's sitting next to a roll of duct tape.

8

gossip and the lazy laundress

Hear no evil, speak no evil. That is my motto . . . except when it comes to gossip. I love it . . . not because I love to spread nasty rumors . . . but because it's where I got my greatest housekeeping idea.

One day my friend came over and sat down on my couch.

"You're never going to believe what I am about to tell you," she said, with a wicked gleam in her eye.

"What?" I said, trying not to sound too interested.

"Well," said my friend, "I was talking to so-and-so and she said that what's-her-name has decided that sorting laundry is a waste of time."

"No," I said, eyes widening.

"Yes," said my friend. "She just throws her whites and darks together, into the same wash load. She thinks if you use cold water the darks won't bleed onto the whites! Can you believe that? Not ever sorting your laundry?"

"Absolutely preposterous!" I said, screwing my face into the proper disapproving frown. But inside I was thinking something much different. Not sorting laundry? Ever again? That is the greatest idea I have ever heard in my entire life!!

I started doing it right away. That very afternoon I unscrupulously tossed white shirts in with dark jeans . . . red socks in with white tights . . . pink pants in with blue panties. What joy! What freedom!

I held my breath as I started the cold wash cycle. I paced back and forth as the clothes tumbled, wondering if I would end up with rainbow underwear. When the washer thumped to a stop, I closed my eyes, lifted out a white shirt and . . . surprise! Nothing happened! What's-her-name was right. An age-old laundry tradition had been broken! A new freedom was born—freedom from the chains of laundry sorting bondage! I felt like I had changed the world!

My husband did not like this new world. He kept imagining that he saw a blue tinge to his white shirts. "Does this look a little funny to you?" he asked me one day, squinting and holding up one of his white Oxford dress shirts.

"Funny?"

"Yeah. It seems like all my white things are turning a little . . . grayish."

"I have no idea what you're talking about," I said, feigning innocence.

Suddenly I heard shrieking. "Moooom!" my daughter yelled, stomping into my bedroom along with my son. "What happened to my t-shirt? It has pink streaks all over it." She looked at her brother. "And will you tell your son to stop wearing pink underwear? The kids are going to make fun of him!"

"I do not have pink underwear . . . it's gray," said my son, holding up a grayish, pinkish pair of formerly white briefs.

My husband glared.

The game was up. I knew when to admit defeat. I told him I had been taking some small shortcuts with the laundry.

"Is this like the shortcut where you stopped matching our socks?" asked my daughter.

"Hey, wasn't I right?" I replied. "No one can see them in your shoes anyway."

"What about when you decided we had to iron our own clothes by sleeping in them?" asked my son.

"Hey, that was efficiency . . . doing two things at once," I said.

"Or how about when your concept for stain removal became, 'If you pretend not to see it, then no one else will either?' " asked my husband, pointing to a spot of old jelly on his pants.

I shrugged. It was true. I did ignore stubborn stains. It was less stressful that way. Besides, "See no evil": that was another one of my housekeeping mottos. And I just knew that someday—it was going to help me revolutionize the laundry-sorting, sock-matching, stain-removing world.

9

stick 'em up

One of the undeniable truths of our earthly existence is that all ten-year-old boys want to be police officers. I find this out when I take ten Cub Scouts on a tour of our local police station. The boys can hardly contain their excitement as they run around pretending to shoot each other with automatic pistols and die horrible deaths. Meanwhile, I try to talk calmly to the receptionist at the window.

"Can I help you?" asks the receptionist, eyes widening when she sees the mayhem that has followed me through the front door.

"Um, yes. We have an appointment," I yell over the din.

"I see," says the receptionist staring at the boy next to me, who has fallen to the floor screaming that he will get even with the man who shot him.

"Too much television," I say, forcing a laugh.

"I see," she replies. "Let me see if Officer Smith is ready for you," and she hastily retreats to the back room.

Two seconds later the side door bursts open and an enormous man in a navy blue uniform towers over the boys.

Immediately, the Cub Scouts, whom I had never seen stop moving, halted in their tracks.

"Well," booms the officer, "I imagine you boys have questions."

Ten hands shoot into the air.

"Officer Smith, have you ever shot anyone?"

"Well now, son, I—"

"Oh, oh, officer, is it true that policemen wear bullet-proof underwear?"

"Not that I, uh—"

"Hey, officer, what's that stick for? Is that what you use to beat people up? Can I try it?"

"Um, no."

Another boy raises his hand. Officer Smith, looking relieved to get to the next question, points to the boy.

"My mother was arrested once . . . she hit a police officer when she was drunk."

Officer Smith is speechless. After a pause, he says, "Oh, well, that's . . . I mean . . . okay, boys, I think it's time to move on to the next room. Follow me."

We follow Officer Smith down a narrow hallway,

the boys peeking into every room and launching question after question.

"Excuse me, Officer, but who was the worst bad guy you ever shot? And what's that thing on the wall?"

"Why son, that is a light switch."

"Does it do anything cool, like electrocute prisoners? I saw on TV where you flip a switch, and the bad guys get electrocuted and all their insides melt. It was so *cool!*"

"COOL!" the other Cub Scouts agree in unison.

Officer Smith looks puzzled. "Well, now . . . I believe it just turns on the lights."

"Oh, you mean the one swinging light bulb that you use to torture confessions out of people?"

Officer Smith frowned. "We don't torture people, boy. What kinds of things have you been watching on television?"

"Is that a *taser* on your belt? Would you shoot it at me? I've always wondered what it feels like."

Officer Smith looks at me. I shrug. One of the boys spots a small door with bars on the windows and runs over to it. The other boys follow. The boy raises his hand as Officer Smith catches up, panting and warning the boys not to touch anything.

"Is this the jail?" the scout asks in a hushed tone. "Is this where you keep all your victims?"

"My what?" says Officer Smith.

"You know, your victims. The ones you shoot, and they don't die. Are there real-live *criminals* behind this door?"

"Listen, son. We do not have victims. We rescue people from criminals. And we don't shoot people."

"Criminals!" says another boy. "Don't you worry, Officer Smith. If any of them try to escape, you catch 'em and we'll tie 'em up. We know lots of knots!"

"Hee, hee." I laugh, as Officer Smith looks at me.

"Yeah," says my son. "And we learned about knives last week. We could make him real nervous by carving soap right in his face!"

"Hey, Officer Smith! Can we pretend to be policemen and put you in jail?"

The boys all start shouting at once.

"I get to use the club!"

"Can I try the siren in your car?"

"What's this mask for? Can I try it on?"

Officer Smith decides to conclude our short tour, making the excuse that he has to get to a meeting.

I look around at my ten happy Cub Scouts as they blissfully tackle and shoot each other while piling into the van. Of all the things I've tried to teach them, at least they've learned one thing: that Boy Scout knots can be used to tie up criminals. Now we can all sleep better at night.

Well, unless you're a criminal. Then you must be very afraid . . . and hide all of your pocket knives and soap in a safe place.

10

hopes and schemes

"Honey . . . !" yells my husband as he stomps toward me down the hallway.

I immediately stop what I am doing. I know that tone of voice. It can only mean one thing: He has discovered one of my elaborate schemes. I have so many of them. It's hard to keep track of which ones he knows about and which ones he has yet to uncover. Quickly, I shuffle through the section of my brain labeled, "Crazy, but Amazing, Plans that Will Irritate My Husband."

Hmm. He sounds wary. I can think of a dozen schemes that might bring on that tone. Perhaps he talked to my best friend at the grocery store this morning. Could she have spilled the beans about how I am going to sneak out of bed and stay up every night until 4 AM, writing cowboy romance novels?

No, I made her pinky promise not to tell anyone

about that, and the fact that I've always wanted to be an opera star. (No one but my shower has heard the beauty with which I sing the role of "Carmen.")

What? I bang the heel of my hand against my forehead. Uh-oh. I bet I forgot to close the Internet site that told about how to raise chickens and a family cow in the back yard. (Hey, I take self-reliance seriously.)

Speaking of self-reliance, maybe he discovered the five hundred pounds of lima beans I bought on sale last week. They were so cheap! I'm positive we can learn to like them.

"Darling," he calls, his voice sounding impatient. "I know you can hear me. Where are you?"

His footsteps are nearing the bedroom where I have flung aside my "How to Re-side Your House in Less than a Day" self-help book, and am pretending to file important papers. My heart beats faster. It sounds serious. Maybe he talked to the lady down the street who set me up with an interview to adopt ten children from Africa. I was going to tell him. I really was. I just wanted to check out all the details first.

"Sweetie."

Gulp. "Hi," I reply in the most innocent, cheerful voice I can muster. "How was your day? Can I get you anything? Newspaper, glass of milk? Sorry we don't serve coffee, but then again—" I clear my throat. "You would know about that because you're Mormon . . . and you . . . um . . . live here too . . . hee hee."

His eyes narrow as I reach up to hug him and then hurry to the bedroom closet.

"Since when have you started fetching my slippers?" he asks, warily holding up his foot so that I can slip off his dress shoe.

I smile my most dazzling smile.

He stares at me, unmoved.

"I need to ask you something important," he says. (Hmm. Maybe I should have used more eye cream last night. Batting my eyelashes doesn't seem to distract him the way it used to . . . Of course, there is always plastic surgery, but that's a scheme for another day . . .)

"Honey, do you have something in your eye?" He peers into my eyeballs. I open them wide, trying to make them sparkle, hoping the bloodshot look they had this morning from my late-night cowboy-novel planning session has disappeared.

His eyebrows lift. He thinks I have finally lost my marbles, I can tell.

"Darling," he says, trying to ignore my enlarged eyeballs. "Did you lose—"

Oh drat! How did he find out about that?

"I didn't mean to!" I wail. "The locksmith gave me a discount when he realized the baby had flushed the keys down the toi—"

"—the receipt for that fishing pole I bought the

other day?" my husband finishes his sentence. He looks confused.

"Locksmith?" he asks.

Oops. Let that be a lesson to you. Communication. Tell your husband everything. *All* your plans and schemes . . . I mean, hopes and dreams. A marriage is not a marriage unless you can sing opera *before* your husband leaves for work. I wonder . . . do you think Madam Butterfly would serve scrambled eggs or cold cereal for breakfast? I guess All-Bran could be a little challenging with chopsticks.

Wait a minute . . . what if my soprano transcends breakfast and moves him so much he wants to whisk me off to an exotic Japanese getaway? Ah-ha . . . but that's a scheme that will never work.

How-ev-er! If I ask for the Galapagos Islands, maybe he'll settle for Disneyland. Yes! I've got to go. I've got plane tickets to research and an elaborate vacation to plan. Sayonara!

11

home alone

There are some things in life that nothing can prepare you for: the wonder of crocus buds in winter, fireworks in the summer sky, the beauty of marriage, holding your first child in your arms, or . . . coming home after leaving your children with a babysitter.

My husband and I lingered in the driveway after our date, watching a gentle rainstorm from the window of our car as it washed over the landscape. We basked in the rare chance to be alone and in love. I gazed at our living room window, thinking fond thoughts of our five children, all nestled sweetly in their beds.

"Oh, honey, look!" I said, pointing. "There's our oldest daughter, sitting in the rocking chair. She must be relaxing and enjoying a book after putting all the kids to bed."

My husband squinted. "I think I see two people in that rocking chair."

I smiled. "Maybe she's rocking the baby to sleep."

"No," my husband replied, opening the car door. "That's not our daughter holding the baby. That is the baby holding the screen off of his bedroom window. How in the world did he get that?"

"What is he doing out of bed?" I wondered aloud as we ran to the front door.

"Mommy!" I was greeted by pounding feet and four wild animals stampeding around the corner. Upon closer inspection, I saw that they were my children.

"Where is your older sister? Isn't she supposed to be watching you?" I asked, trying to stay calm when I noticed what looked like tattoos all over my eight-year-old daughter.

"It's jewelry, Mom," she explained. "You said I couldn't play with yours, so I drew my own. I even have a nose ring. See?"

"Where is your sister?" demanded my husband in a quiet voice. His words were slow and controlled. Boy, those stress-management techniques I learned at Home, Family, and Personal Enrichment were really working for him.

"She went to bed," answered my four-year-old, giving us a chubby-cheeked grin. "She said she was tired of trying to keep the hooly-mans in bed."

"Hooligans," corrected my ten-year-old.

"What in the world?" growled my husband, pluck-

41

ing the baby off of the window screen. Our toddler was covered from head to toe in Band-Aids. His eyes were the only things not taped shut.

"Oh, that," explained my ten-year-old son. "He wanted me to bandage all of his 'owies' after we got him out of bed."

"What 'owies'? What were you doing getting him out of bed?"

"He got them from sliding down the blanket slide we made off of the top bunk," my daughter piped in. When she saw the look on our faces she added, "Don't worry—we were holding onto the blankets real tight!"

"You sent him down a blanket slide? What were you thinking? He could've been—"

"Killed . . . I know!" said my older son. "That's what we were worried about when we saw the lightning. We were holding fire drills, in case of a fire. We wanted to practice how we would shoot him to safety if we had to save him. We were just about to practice sliding him out the window when you got home."

My husband stiffened. Then he sniffed the air, "Is that smoke I smell?"

"Oh, yeah. Sorry about that," said my son. "We wanted to test out the smoke detector to see if it was working, so we microwaved a spoon."

Safety first, that's the motto in our family. My husband and I sighed. We couldn't complain. Our kids were using creative ingenuity to solve their own problems. Still, I decided that on our next date night we would find a way to romantically count the dots on the door to our microwave, protecting it and the baby from the ingenuity of our other children. Now . . . if only I could figure out how to remove a nose ring and several hundred bracelets, drawn in permanent marker. Hmmm. Maybe I could cover them up with Band-Aids.

12

the church bag

It's 9 AM on Sunday morning. We've just screeched into the church parking lot. My husband shouts out orders: "Son, you run and get us a seat. You, carry in all the scriptures, and you—" he points at our teenage daughter, "—grab the baby."

He hands the toddler to me and tries to pick up the church bag. "Ugh. What is in this thing? I can't even lift it out of the car."

I look at the bag. It's big and lumpy with pencils and papers sticking out of several holes in the bottom corners.

"Just stuff that we need in church," I reply. "Do you want me to carry it?"

"No," he grunts, "I can get it." He hoists it onto his back and begins to trudge toward the church.

"Don't forget to grab the blankie and the pacifier," I call out over my shoulder. "And I brought some coloring books for the kids."

My husband grumbles under his breath as he drags the bag back to the car and grabs the necessary paraphernalia.

"Don't forget to grab the diapers and wipes under the front seat," I say, turning around to see if he's all right.

He looks like a pack llama, and he is dropping things left and right. Muttering, he finally catches up to me by the door.

"Did you get the sippy cup?" I ask sweetly.

He glares at me. Shrugging, I walk through the glass doors of the church. As I walk and he waddles down the hall, people stop us.

"Are you okay?"

"Can I give you hand with that?"

My husband shakes his head, his face red. He is out of breath and unable to speak.

Finally we reach our seats. With a loud thump and an enormous clatter he drops the church bag and everything else he is carrying next to our pew. Sitting down next to me, he leans over and whispers, "I know this is a dumb question. But may I ask what the purpose of a church bag is, if you can't fit the church stuff inside of it? "

I sigh. "You'll be glad I brought everything when the kids start whining."

"Humph," he grumbles, digging through the bag. "What is this? You have every church bulletin in here since 1993!"

Grinning, I respond, "Hey, there are phone numbers on those papers that we might need someday."

The baby starts to fuss. "Find him a toy, will you?" I ask.

My husband digs through the mounds of church bulletins and pulls out a half-eaten bagel. "When is the last time you cleaned this thing out?" he whispers.

Digging deeper he finds an old lesson manual, twenty-six "Smarties" wrappers, a dirty diaper, and five broken pencils.

Finally, he strikes gold. He holds up a headless Barbie.

"You can't give him that to play with in church," I hiss.

My husband looks confused as I shove the doll back into the bag. "She's not dressed modestly. What will the Bankses think when they see our son playing in the pew with a half-dressed Barbie doll?"

"Fine," he grumps, heaving the church bag in my direction and taking the baby. "You find something for him to play with."

"Fine," I reply. I bite my lip, trying to remember what is lurking beneath all of those church bulletins. Aha! I know one way to find out. Lifting up the corner of the bag, I stick my finger into one of the holes and yank out a pen. Then I uncrumple a church bulletin and give it to the baby to draw on. The baby squeals contentedly as he chews on the pen and rips up the bulletin.

I smile at my husband. "It's a good thing I keep this old bag. Those holes at the bottom are pretty handy."

"Yeah. Pure genius," my husband replies.

After sacrament meeting, my visiting teacher stops by our pew. Her eyebrows rise as she takes in the mayhem that has spilled out of our lumpy old bag. Hiding her dismay, she offers to take my church bag home and organize it for me.

"Organize?" I laugh. "This is organized!" I say, meaning it. I'm the most organized person I know. "Go ahead," I tell her. "Ask me for the phone number of the missionaries who lived here in 1997. I bet there is no one else in this ward who has that information."

She smiles and nods politely before edging away. I stand up and heave the bag onto my shoulder. I just hope I can coax some old Smarties to fall out of the holes in the bottom for my primary class. There's nothing like a bribe to help those sunbeams sit in their chairs.

See? Good old church bag. If you leave it long enough, there'll be stuff in there to solve all of your problems. Don't ever clean it, and don't ever leave home without it.

13

the best birthday present ever!

My son's second birthday is coming up, and I've thought of the perfect present! This toy is every parent's dream. It is a water toy that comes in one piece so there are no parts to keep track of. It is simple and doesn't require any adult help to operate. Not only that, this toy is creative and has dozens of possibilities and applications both in and out of the water. But its most important feature is that there is absolutely no assembly required. What is this amazing invention that will keep every toddler amused for hours and hours? It's a toilet brush.

I'm not joking. I've tried giving two-year-olds other toys, but after the joy of ripping open the packages and strewing the pieces all over the house (and inserting them into every hole they can find including the VCR, heating vent, and their sleeping father's mouth), they lose interest. This is because children do not actually like toys. Stores and television commercials may make toys seem exciting, but no toy will ever be able to compete with a two-year-old's favorite activity, which is playing in the toilet. Think about it: you push a lever and water sprays everywhere, making a huge noise, which then brings your mother running . . . especially when you dump a whole bag of breakfast cereal in first.

Then there are the accessories that come with it, such as toilet paper. Toilet paper has endless creative possibilities.

Who can resist the urge to pull the little tail of paper, whirling the roll around and around until you are up to your knees in glorious, soft, white fluffiness? (I have to admit the urge to spin the roll with abandon has even hit me on the odd occasion.)

And oh . . . the things you can wrap. You wrap your legs, your torso, your arms, your head, twirling and twirling, and then—you spy the cat. Ha ha! You squeal with delight as you tear after him, tripping and falling over your tied up legs, and then scrambling back up like a feline's worst nightmare. Here kitty, kitty! Until your mother comes running to see what the noise is all about, and she scoops you up in her arms, laughing, as you try to wrap her in waves of soft, cottony delight.

Once again, the cat has escaped my little two-year-old feline terrorist, and he is lucky. This is because his tail has the misfortune of being the second favorite child's toy in our house. How can they resist that fuzzy flag, waving merrily, and disappearing and reappearing among the jungle of tables and chairs. It seems to say, "Catch me if you can."

Yes, there is no toy that can compete with a toilet, a tail, or the next best thing—a daddy. A daddy is a wonderful thing. A human jungle gym that you can climb and slide down. There is hair to pull, cheeks to pinch, eyes to poke, and teeth to inspect. When he is sleeping, my children like to play a ring toss game, using his nose as the peg. But the current favorite is to pull his eyelids open and inspect the whites of his eyeballs, yelling loudly, "Daddy, are you sleeping?" over and over until he grabs the child and throws him up in the air, growling like a great big papa bear woken from his nap. This inevitably leads to a game of "Wee-ha's" in which the children are thrown over the daddy's head in various complex flips and jumps worthy of Olympic fame.

There will never be a toy boat or train, or any toy truck, that can compete with a daddy's eyeball or a toilet with all its accessories. This is why I am getting my son a toilet scrub brush for his birthday. At least he can be cleaning when he gets into trouble, splashing in the toilet or brushing a yowling cat.

That gives me a great idea for my four-year-old's birthday present! A wire coat hanger. This is the perfect accessory to her favorite toy . . . chewing gum. Maybe while she is thinking of all the endless creative possibilities, she can also use it to pry off the wads of gum that she has stuck into all of the nooks and crannies of her bedroom. Then again, maybe not. I just remembered she'll probably try and use it on her second favorite toy . . . her two-year-old brother.

14

new year's resolution

This is the year I will get organized. I will clean up that five foot high mound of coats by the front door. I will no longer store spaghetti sauce with the kids' underwear. No more crusty gooey stains on the shelves of my refrigerator. I will (gulp) fold clothes. And last but not least . . . I vow to rid my world of all knicknack items. That is why I have turned into "High-Strung, Fierce Junk Annihilator Mommy."

Day 1: I rush to the store and buy forty-eight clear plastic organizing boxes, one in every size. People stare as I drive behind a ceiling-high stack of boxes in my cart, dragging five whiney kids on my pant legs. I apologize to anyone I run down, but they can't hear me over the din of children begging for things.

Day 2: I organize the kitchen. All food items are stored alphabetically, every pan is assigned a home, and I have gotten rid of all "superfluous" items previously stored on the top of the refrigerator, such as our ping pong ball set, two science fiction novels, last year's banana bread from Aunt Hilda, my son's lint collection, and our tax returns. (Hey, where else am I going to store them?)

Day 3: No one is allowed into the kitchen.

Kids: "But, Moooooom, we're hungry!"

Me: "Sorry. If I cook, then I will mess up my alphabetical system."

Son: "Hey, what happened to that special bowl I made for you in my school art class?"

Me: "Um . . . eeer . . ."

Daughter (shrieking from the other room): "Mooom! Why are my dolls in the garbage?"

Me: "Because your brother pulled off all their heads."

Daughter: "So? I love these dolls. You can't throw them away . . . Hey, what's this?" (She lifts up a soggy mass of grayish material)

Baby: "My blankie! My blankie!"

Son (accusingly): "You threw away your own son's blankie?"

Me (squirming): "Well . . . it looked . . . superfluous."

Five minutes later the garbage was emptied, the cupboards were raided for food, and my alphabetical system was ruined. Oh well. At least this New Year's resolution lasted one day longer than last year's. I wonder what I can do with forty-eight clear plastic boxes.

15

the golden age

Some people call eighteen months old the golden age of babyhood. Finally your baby can do more than just spit and cry. He makes wonderful discoveries such as how the length of an entire roll of toilet paper will reach all the way down to the basement when unrolled properly. He rewards all your self-sacrifice as a mother by preferring his father over you. He loves to see how far into the living room he can fling his cereal bowl. And even though you would shun most people for this type of anti-social behavior, somehow when your own child does it, all you can say is, "Isn't that adorable?"

But beware. This adorable behavior is a trap. My husband and I call it the "Sucker Season" of babyhood. It happens every time. Our baby turns eighteen months old, and after a particularly golden afternoon when our child has performed many great acts of sublime cuteness, I look at my husband and say, "Let's have another one."

My husband drops his fork. He looks at me long and hard. I realize he is too moved to speak. Yes, I can see that he is so touched he is crying . . . he can't speak . . . no wait . . . he's choking on his food. He is signing to me that he can't breathe.

I whack him hard on the back and dislodge the piece of tuna casserole that was stuck in his throat. Finally he is ready to speak. He takes both of my hands in his. He looks deep into my eyes and says . . .

"Are you out of your ever-living mind?"

"Do you not remember," says he, "that just eighteen short months ago you built a huge bonfire in our back yard and burned all of your maternity clothes while dancing around the flames and shouting that you would never look at another hot dog as long as you lived?'

"Yes, but—"

"And have you forgotten," he cries, "how sick you got after you went crazy and ate thirty-six deviled eggs in one night?"

"Twenty-six actually—"

"And what about last night," he recalls, "when you told the kids who wouldn't go to bed that you were moving to Siberia and never coming back?"

"I never said . . ."

"You did."

"Okay, okay," I say, raising my hands in defeat. "But have *you* forgotten, that all those hot dog cravings resulted in these five beautiful children, whom you've held, and rocked, and snuggled, and sang to, and bathed, and burped, and loved, until they absolutely adore you? How can you not want another one of them?" I ask, pointing to our beautiful descendents who are now shouting at each other and pretending to feed their tuna casserole to the dog, even though we don't have a dog. At that moment, our eighteen-month-old flings a noodle into my husband's eye. This time my husband really is crying.

"Adorable!" I say.

"Adorable" he says, "but before you commit to having another one of these adorable little rascals, I'd like you to put the kids to bed . . . by yourself."

"Okay," I say. "I'm tough. I can do it. What will you be doing?"

"I thought I'd make you a little treat. You're going to need your strength . . ."

"Treat? Why, sweetheart! What are you making?"

"Thirty-six deviled eggs. I just wanted you to relive some of the good old days. Plus, after the kids go to bed, you might need them."

"Need them? For what?"

"Your trip to Siberia."

16

sloppy halloween

My husband always says, "If something is worth doing, it's worth doing right." I disagree. My philosophy is . . . get in there and get the experience any way you can. Even if it's terrible, at least you've done it. Take this Halloween for instance. My friend spent hours carefully bundling each of her kids up so they wouldn't be shivering while trick-or-treating outside at our church carnival. By the time she was done, they had missed the carnival and all her kids were crying.

I, on the other hand, looked up at the clock and realizing that we were late, kicked all my kids into the car in various states of undress.

Daughter: "But, Moooooom, what about my other shoe?"

Me: "Here, wear this one"

Daughter: "But that's your shoe. It's way too big."

Me: "Listen, kid, do you want candy or not?"

Son: "Mom, Mom, Mom, Mom! I lost my pirate patch. I can't go without the eye patch! I won't look like a pirate."

Me: "Here, wear this over your eye."

Son: "Huh? But that's one of the blueberry pancakes we had for dinner."

Me: "I know. I know. But just think, you'll be able to have a little snack to eat if you get hungry."

When we arrived at the carnival, I took my kids around to the various trick-or-treat stations and barely avoided getting arrested by several clucking grandmothers.

Clucking grandmothers: "Are you trying to freeze your baby to death? Where are his mittens?"

Me: "You're right. Here, I'll fix it by putting his socks on his hands. There!"

Clucking grandmothers: "But now his *feet* are freezing."

Me: "Hey, he's happy. He's chewing on five different types of candy at once. The euphoria produces a warming effect."

Daughter (pulling on my leg): "Mom, I'm cold. When are we going home?"

Clucking grandmothers (nodding and pursing their lips at me in triumph).

Me: "What? She likes to be miserable. Look. She's shivering with excitement and delight."

Unfortunately, at that point, all five of my children

converged on me at once and started to whine about being cold, so I high-tailed it out of there before those grandmothers could handcuff me.

When we arrived home it was time to carve pumpkins, and all of a sudden I thought, "Do you *really* have to scrape out all the slimy stuff before you cut the face out? Or is that just a silly tradition?" And so, after pretending to scoop out some of the seeds, I carved out the five hundred teeth the kids drew on their pumpkins, and they didn't even notice the slimy orange, hangy things behind the eyes. Except for my son, and he liked it—"Cool, Mom. You made my pumpkin have a runny nose!"

After this warm praise, I created more happy memories by serving our traditional homemade doughnuts and hot chocolate, which this year turned out to be carrot sticks and some old tomato juice since my husband was out of town and couldn't help me.

I was just patting myself on the back for giving my kids the Halloween experience, even though there were a few short cuts, when the doorbell rang.

Trick-or-Treater: "Um, ma'am. You might want to come outside. Your Halloween pumpkins are on fire."

Oops. I guess that was the reason we were supposed to scrape out all of the slimy stuff. Ah, well. You win some, you lose some. Hey, I wonder if I've just discovered a revolutionary way to toast pumpkin seeds! Pass the salt.

17

sock it to 'em

Sports are my husband's life. Eating and sleeping are a burden when they get in the way of college football. To him the basic building blocks of life are baseball, football, basketball, and soccer. This is why when my ten-year-old son looks up from his mashed potatoes at dinner one night and says, "I love it when Dad comes to our soccer games. He helps us win," I grow suspicious.

Me: "What do you mean 'helps you win'?"

Son: "You know. He yells out stuff."

Me: "He yells? Do the coaches get mad?"

Son: "Nah. But that's because Dad knows way more than the coaches do."

I look over at my husband. He shrugs, saying, "I can't help it. When you know more about the principles of the game than the coaches, you've got to speak up. I can't let the kids lose."

I decide right then and there that I need to start

attending my son and daughter's soccer games. Luckily they are on the same team.

As the coaches are setting up for the game, I observe my two children's pregame rituals. My son begins to psych up for the game with an intense ritual called, "Run around and bug the heck out of the coaches."

"Can I be goalie?"

"No."

"Why not?"

"Because."

"But I love goalie."

"No."

"Pleeeeease?"

"No."

"C'mon, you gotta let me be goalie."

"I said no. Hey, look up there. Is that an alien space ship?"

"Huh? Hey, wait, don't run away. I gotta ask you something . . ."

My daughter, on the other hand, starts her pregame ritual with something much more challenging: ballerina pirouettes around the goal post. Actually this is her method of playing soccer. It works too! My husband said in the last game she took out two eight-year-olds with one of her double jete leaps. Unfortunately, they were her own team members.

The game starts. I notice my husband biting his lip.

His forehead begins to sweat. He is trying to restrain himself. My son runs around like a streak of lightning, stealing the ball from his own teammate and kicking it into the goal. He is taken out of the game for too much celebration. I have to admit, falling to one knee and reaching for the sky is a bit much.

My husband explodes. "What! I can't believe it."

I shake my head, trying to hide under my stadium blanket.

The other team gets the ball, and all the kids congregate into one massive jumble of arms and legs moving up and down the field with the ball . . . except for my daughter, who is playing "Rock, Paper, Scissors" with herself in the backfield.

My husband can't stop himself. He leaps out of his lawn chair and follows the mass of flailing arms and legs up and down the field yelling out advice. "Get it, Tommy. Don't let the ball get past you! Stay with it, guys."

I have to admit, it is rather exciting even though no one can actually tell where the ball is.

Finally, the referee blows the whistle, when it is discovered that there *is* no ball in the middle of the running mass of children. It popped out of bounds early on and was stolen by a big white dog who is now sitting on the sidelines, chewing it to death.

The referee grabs the slobbery ball and gives it to the other team.

I stand up and yell, "Hey, what do you mean? That was a white dog. It should be the dark team's ball."

My husband looks at me in shock. I shrug. Hey, somebody's gotta give the referee advice. He obviously has trouble with colors. Doesn't he know you're not supposed to wear white socks with black shoes? And those stripes are just calling attention to his problem areas. I can't help it. When you know more about the principles of fashion than the referee, you just gotta speak up. Maybe next year I'll suggest a soft sage green for the kid's uniforms. That navy blue is doing nothing for my son's delicate skin tone.

18

i'm tied up in knots

When you volunteer to be a new Cub Scout leader, they give you this really helpful manual. What they don't tell you is that nobody in their right mind uses it. This is because the ideas in the manual are meant to be a joke on new Cub Scout leaders. Take this month's theme for instance: rope tying. Who was the wise guy who came up with the idea of letting ten-year-old boys play with rope? Being new, I decide to try it, not foreseeing the obvious problems.

My first clue that this lesson is going to be a disaster comes when I begin with a question.

Me: "Who can tell me some useful purposes for this rope?"

Cub Scout #1: "Tying up your sister?"

Me: "Now, John, is that really useful?"

Cub Scout #2: "How about strangling your cat?"

Me: "Nooooo. I don't think so . . ."

Cub Scout #3: "Oooo, I know, I know. Hanging people?"

Me: "Never mind. Let's just get on with the lesson."

Against my better judgment, I hand each boy a length of rope. Then I begin to teach the boys all about knots . . . which is a problem, since I don't really know how to tie any. I had practiced with the helpful illustrations at home, but somehow, I can't remember anything but the rectangle knot . . . or was it the triangle?

Me: "Okay, boys, here's how you tie a Double Half-Hilch, er, Full-Hilch? No, it's a half-hoax. You take the right side and cross it over the left, then you loop it around like so . . . and ta da! Um, well it was supposed to work. Just a minute, let me figure this out."

Danny: "Don't you mean the half-hitch? You tie it like this." (His fingers whirl around, expertly tying a perfect knot).

Me: "Er . . . well. Yes, right. Could you do that one more time?"

While I try to get Danny to show me the fence post hitch something or other, the boys entertain themselves by choking each other with their ropes.

Me: "Tommy, stop choking Sam with that rope. Jimmy, why are you crying?"

Jimmy: "Because he [nodding toward my son] handcuffed me with his rope and I can't move."

My son: "I was just trying to practice the square knot you taught us."

Out of the corner of my eye I see one boy chasing another, twirling a crudely-tied lasso, and I realize it's time to distract the boys with a game. I teach them how to coil a rope and attach a weight to the end in order to rescue someone who has fallen off a cliff. The boys think this is really neat. My first volunteer has trouble getting up because another boy has tied his leg to a chair. After several failed attempts to untangle his knots, I finally make him drag his leg with the chair up to the top of our pretend "cliff."

Carefully, he coils up the rope just like I showed him, aims, and throws the rope toward the boy who is being "rescued," hitting him squarely in the forehead with the heavy weight. The boy wasn't able to jump out of the way because he had tied his own two legs together while waiting for me to untie the other Cub Scout.

Unfortunately, we aren't learning first aid until next month, so I do the best I can to check for lumps, and then I untie all the boys from each other, delivering them more or less in one piece to their mothers. I realize that I am a failure as a Cub Scout leader.

That night my son comes up to me and shows me the knots he has been practicing all evening, saying, "Mom, I love Cub Scouts. It teaches you really useful things."

I look at his knots, which are tied all wrong, but just

like I showed him. Well, I guess it doesn't matter if his bowline looks more like a bow-mess. At least he thinks he learned something, and he had fun doing it. Gee, I can't wait for the "carving with pocketknives" lesson.

19

one heck of a haircut

Nothing will bring more opinionated people out of the woodwork than a new haircut. I once went to a new hairdresser with a magazine picture of Christie Brinkley. "Make me look like that," I commanded, slapping the clipping on the counter. I decided to bring a picture this time because no matter how many different ways I get my hair cut, it always looks the same when I try to style it at home: a stringy-looking bob with two cowlicks on top.

My new hairdresser did not mince words. He studied the clipping, examined a few strands of my graying hair, and then ripped up the picture.

"Impossible," he decreed with hand gestures and an Italian accent.

I must have looked crestfallen, because he then said in a gentler voice, "Listen. You've gotta worka with what you've been given. Don't worry. I will fix everything."

Then he grinned and snapped his scissors at me with a maniacal gleam in his eye.

"Excuse me," I squeaked, "what do you mean by fix everyth—"

"Silence!" he shouted, glaring and spinning my chair to face the mirror. "Never interrupt an *artiste* at work."

Meekly, I slumped in my chair and watched the flurry of scissors and flying hair until . . .

"AHA!" he shouted in triumph. "Whata do you think of *this*?"

He spun my chair around and I saw in the mirror what looked to be a really, really *short* stringy-looking bob with two cowlicks on top. I looked like a chipmunk . . . with bangs.

When I got home I found out there are many different forms of honesty.

1. There was my daughter who took one look at me and ran away screaming, "You're not my Mommy!"

2. My husband looked up from his dinner and asked, "Can't that darn hairdresser find someone else's hair to experiment on?"

3. My son grinned. "I like it!" Then he held out his hand, "Can I have twenty dollars?"

4. My mother hugged me and said, "We love you no matter what you look like, dear."

5. The grocery store clerk took one look at my short hair and asked, "Mid-life crisis?"

At church, the ladies gathered around me saying things like, "Oooo you're hair!" and "Wow, that's different."

I took these comments to be positive because they were better than the ones I received after one of my previous haircuts. In a desperate attempt to achieve a newer, younger look I had tried to cut my own hair, using my sharpest kitchen shears and a bathroom mirror. It turned out looking suspiciously like a reverse-mullet.

After that haircut my own children wouldn't claim me as their mother, and grocery store ladies whispered as they walked by, "What happened to the back of her head?"

Which is why this time, when my best friend noticed my new haircut and said, "It's sassy!" I knew I had found the right hairdo. Who cares if bangs went out of style with the cavemen? To heck with Christie Brinkley . . . If I was going to look like a chubby, middle-aged chipmunk with bangs, I would do it with style! Besides, you've gotta worka with what you've been given, right?

20

shop 'til you drop

An unfortunate side effect of having five children is the need to go shopping. This is because in order for your children to survive, they require necessities such as two hundred "Dora" videos, a freezer full of frozen pizza, and eight pairs of designer pants that cost as much as a car.

One thing children need a lot of is school supplies. Schools carefully put together a detailed list of items your child will need. The list will contain such things as a vinyl folder with eight pockets, which is not sold in any store. Teachers put this item on the list to test the child's parents for the ability to come up with creative solutions. After the parent has searched twelve stores in three different towns with five screaming children will they:

1. Cave in and buy a folder with only *seven* pockets?

2. Fashion their own eight pocket folder using mud flaps and man's greatest invention: duct tape.

The results of this test help the teachers know where to seat your child in the classroom: children with innovative parent geniuses to the front, children with parents who are dumb as a post to the back.

I took this helpful school supply list and my five children to the store the other day. I had the insane idea that it might be more efficient to shop with all the children at once. The day went something like this . . . .

Son: "Mom, I *have* to have those superhero notebooks."

Me: "But they cost ten dollars each."

Son: "I know, but it says right here on the list, 'Superhero notebooks.' "

Me: "Let me see that list . . ."

Daughter: "Mom, Mom, Mom, Mom, Mom, you have to buy me this pink lunch box. I will die if anyone sees my lunch box from last year."

Me: "What's wrong with last year's lunch box?"

Toddler: "Wunch Box . . . I waaaaaant a wunch booooox!"

Son: "Mom, is it okay if the baby is climbing up the store shelves?"

Me (sighing): "Just make sure he's wearing a safety helmet."

Son: "What? Mom . . . you need a nap. I'm going to look at the basketballs."

Teenager: "I will NOT wear these shoes! They make me look fat. I don't understand why I can't have the shoes that cost a whole year's salary. What good is money if it just sits around in the bank?"

Intercom: "Would the owner of a ten-year-old child with the last name of Campbell please come to the service desk and pay for the expensive lamps that he just knocked over?"

Me (to the staring crowd beginning to form a circle around my cart): "Sheesh! Don't you wish some parents would keep a closer eye on their children?"

Daughter: "Mom, why do they keep saying our last name over the loud speaker?"

I slink away from the crowd, making a bee line for the service center where I pick up my sheepish looking son.

Me: "What were you doing? You were gone for twenty seconds."

Son: "I just wanted to see if a lamp shade would make a good basketball hoop. Have you found my eight pocket folder yet?"

Me (thinking): *I wonder if this place sells duct tape . . .*

We finally head to the checkout where I try to sprint through the line before my kids can loot all of the candy which has been deviously placed at their eye-level.

Me: "Put that gum back on the shelf, sweetie."

Daughter: "But Moooooooooooooooooooooom! Why can't I haaave it?"

Me: "Because, dear, you know your doctor said you can't have anything artificially sweetened. It might re-trigger that dreadfully contagious disease you're just getting over."

This little white lie always gets me through the checkout fast.

When we load the $346 worth of supplies into the car, I realize I have forgotten to purchase a twenty-five cent ruler. I assure my daughter it will be okay. We'll just fashion something out of flattened toilet paper tubes and duct tape. No child of mine is going to be sitting in the back row of the classroom.

21

the best intentions . . .

In this ever-changing world there are only two things that are inevitable: Death and Muffin-top. In mentioning the latter, I, of course, refer to the extra spillage of the middle section over the top of the ever-shrinking waistband as your birthdays begin to spiral even faster toward the three digit mark. Unless, of course, the former gets you first . . . which could, in part, be caused by the latter. These two certainties will then ultimately cause the third and final inevitability, which is that husbands will always hate their birthdays, no matter what you do to cheer them up.

At least that is what I thought when I decided to distract my husband from his age by throwing him the biggest, most fabulous birthday celebration ever conceived upon the face of the earth. I was sure that the atmosphere of family, food, friends, and music would make him feel appreciated for the amazing husband and father that he was . . . and I hoped that he wouldn't be too put out by the cost of the clown, the zip-line, the Dixie-land band, and twenty-foot high jumpy castle either.

Unfortunately, I ran into some problems right from the start.

"You want $150 for ten minutes of jumping? What kind of a . . . don't you have any kind of economy packages? Oh, you've got jump ropes for fifty cents? I'll take twenty."

And later . . .

"What do you mean Bumpo the clown is on sabbatical? When will he be back? In five to twenty? Well, I guess I could *ask* my husband if he wanted to have his party at the county jail."

And later . . .

"Mom, mom, mom! Can we help mix the batter? Please? What's this? I'll pour it in."

"No, I want to!"

"No me!"

"Kids, STOP! That's flea powder, not sugar!"

And much, much later . . .

"Mom, don't cry. I didn't mean to step in the middle of the cake. Dad will still like it. It will remind him of his kids."

"Yeah," I replied, sinking into a chair and putting my chin in my hands. I had failed. This party was not going anywhere: No cake, no music, and no friends . . .

just a whole lot of jump ropes.

Later that night my husband came home.

"Daddy! Happy Birthday! We made your favorite dinner: Cheetos and milk!"

My husband looked at me.

I bit my lip and stared at the ground, digging my toe into a hole in the linoleum. "Um, yeah. Sorry about that. I forgot to thaw out the T-bone last night."

My eight-year-old daughter pulled on her father's pant leg, her face alive with excited anticipation. "Daddy, Daddy, open my present first!"

My husband sat down at the table and began opening up a lopsided, pink, homemade paper box.

"Wow," he said, his eyes twinkling. "I love it."

"What is it? What is it?" yelled my other four children, climbing over each other to get a closer look.

My husband dumped out twelve smooth grey rocks, stolen from our neighbor's flower garden.

"It's a whole bunch of little paperweights," said my husband, sounding as if this was what he'd always dreamed of receiving on his birthday.

"No, Daddy," replied my daughter with impatience. "It's a puzzle. You have to see what it says."

My husband tried arranging the wobbly-looking letters that had been painstakingly drawn on each rock. Apparently, my daughter had lost track of her spelling during the creative process, because after several tries at reorganization my husband finally read, "H-A-P-P-Y B-A-R-F-D-A-Y! "

That did it. We all collapsed in guffaws until we could breathe no longer. Then, after stuffing our bellies full of Cheetos, we decided to bring out the cake. My husband read the message on the cake out loud with a grin.

"Happy Birthday, Dear Rachel." He looked up at me. "Wow, honey! Thanks!"

I gave him a sheepish smile. "I found it in the freezer from last month's party. Our first cake didn't turn out so well . . . ."

Finally, it was time to open my present. My husband eagerly slipped the vinyl-covered book out of the bag. Then he paused.

"Gee. I've always wanted *Lovin' Dutch Ovens*! Thanks so much!"

He leaned over and whispered to me out of the corner of his mouth. "Honey. I don't have a dutch oven."

I ground my teeth together. "I know. I know. Sorry. I got to the sporting goods store just after they locked their doors. I tried to be obnoxious and bribe the manager to let me in, but he told me to quit being a public nuisance." I slouched down in my kitchen chair, pouting.

My husband laughed and pulled me over for a much needed hug.

"Guess it wasn't such a great birthday, huh?" I asked, my voice muffled in the shoulder I loved so much.

Not wanting to be left out, my kids ran over and squeezed in between our bodies for a group snuggle.

"Daddy," said my four-year-old. "I can hear your heart beeping."

My husband laughed. "Don't you mean beating?" he asked. Then he continued, "That's because I am the happiest, most blessed Dad in the world, and this was the best birthday ever!"

I smiled, and we embraced each other harder around our muffin-top middles. (I knew there was a reason we needed those jump ropes.) I guess I forgot to mention the other certainty in this life: that I would love this most amazing man for the rest of eternity. Happy Barf-day, sweetheart! I love you.

22

attack of the dust mites

There is a serious energy crisis in America. Every evening parents fall into bed, too tired to pick up the old pieces of toast and clothing that have been strewn about the floor of their homes.

The creators of this nation-wide energy deficit are tiny creatures commonly known as—your kids. Each day you follow them around, carefully removing their droppings, such as backpacks and wet towels, so that they are free to make messes in other parts of the house.

The other day my son came home from school, threw his backpack on the floor, opened the fridge, and took everything out in order to find an old can of chocolate frosting. Then, leaving everything on the counter, he spread the frosting on a cracker, wiped his fingers on the curtains, and went into the living room to spread chocolate frosting cracker crumbs all over the carpet.

I let him do this because I was trying to determine if he was an evil spirit who was trying to destroy our house on purpose, or if he just didn't notice the automatic lowering of our house's market value by one thousand dollars every time he entered a room.

That's when it hit me. Perhaps the solution to this nation's energy crisis existed right in our own home. Perhaps this solution was, at this moment, playing computer games and dropping bubble gum wrappers on the floor of my very own living room.

That's right. You guessed it! Child labor. C'mon, admit it. You know it was your sole motivation for having children. Don't you remember the tender age when you discovered that doing work was the only reason your parents had you?

The idea of your kids doing the housework has many advantages. For example:

1. Your son will vacuum your living room until it is done, approximately three vacuum passes later.

2. When your teenage daughter cleans the bathroom you will have peace of mind knowing that there are five fewer germs on the toilet seat from the one swipe she made with the cloth.

3. Children can do each small job in just under six hours.

4. You can spend more time with your children because you will have to harass your son for hours to keep him focused on his task of feeding the fish.

"Feed the fish, son."

"Okay, dad . . . but what's that screw for?"

"Keep your focus, son. You can do it. Pick up the bag."

"Dad, have you ever seen a poison dart frog? We have one in our classroom—"

"The *bag*, son. THE BAG!"

"Okay, but where do babies come from?"

Even your toddler can be useful. He can put away all the clean silverware in the wrong places so that you can keep your brain sharp in its old age by hunting for your breakfast spoon every morning.

Of course, the best job to assign to your children is raking leaves. This is because the child will spend ten hours raking the whole yard, only to go back to the first tree and find that it has dropped thousands more leaves since he last raked under it. This effectively keeps the children working outside "forever" so that they won't be messing up the inside of your house.

Despite the many advantages of this system, there is one inherent problem with using children to do your "dirty" work: *Children are experts at job avoidance.*

"No."

"But I'm scared."

"I'm right here, there's nothing to be scared of."

"But what if a bear comes?"

"There are no bears."

"What about bats?"

"The tent is zipped."

"A centipede could get in."

"There are no centipedes. Will you please be quiet and go to sleep?"

After a moment of silence, I hear a scuffle.

"Ouch. Dad, she stepped on me."

"Did not!"

"Did too!"

"That's it!" roars my husband. "Either you all get back in your sleeping bags, or I'm kicking everybody out of this tent!"

I unzip my window and watch as flashlights and shadows of arms and legs flash and flail all over their tent. At one point, I can identify the silhouette of a child pressed against the side of the tent, screaming and looking like a frozen Han Solo from *The Empire Strikes Back*.

After a long, agonizing night, I realize that camping is great for the kids, but exhausting for the parents. Still, besides the heat, bugs, germs, injuries, dirt, whining, and lack of sleep, it was kind of fun. I can't wait to go again next year.

24

germ-o-phobia

I have five beautiful, active, feisty, roll-in-the-mud, get-down-and-get-dirty children, and my best friend is a germaphobe.

The fact that we are friends at all is a miraculous phenomenon beyond our ability to comprehend. I am not exaggerating when I say her house is so clean you could eat poached eggs out of the bathtub. Her children are happy, loved, and immaculately well cared for. My children are happy, loved, and really, really lucky to make it out of the house without oatmeal stuck to the front of their shirts.

My house is so conducive to germs from five kids touching everything that we are now being researched by experts for new and exciting mutant strains of bacteria. No, just kidding. But we do have mold experiments growing in our fridge. Needless to say, get-togethers can be a challenge.

"Are you *sure* you want to ride in my car to the museum today?" I ask my friend, thinking of the gum I am going to have to scrape off of the back of the driver's seat before she sees it. She is standing on my doorstep with her kids in her car, not ready to unleash them into my lone and germy world without supervision.

My best friend takes a deep breath. I think she is performing Yoga breathing exercises to psych herself up for the experience. She closes her eyes. "Yes, I can do it." She opens her eyes and sees that my toddler has wandered up to wipe his nose on my pants.

"I-I-I'll just get my kids out of the car . . ." she stutters, backing away.

"Okay. If you're sure. I'll meet you in my garage," I reply. I snatch up my little one and madly run for the vacuum cleaner. I've got to vacuum up two inches of cracker crumbs out of my toddler's car seat. If my friend knew my toddler looked on that pile as her emergency stash of snack food, we might end up making a trip to the hospital for cardiac arrest.

I open up the garage door after I've done a quick car clean up. She is standing stiffly, holding her children close. She tries to navigate through the pile of toys and bikes in the garage next to our van. Her son bends over to inspect a mud-encrusted soccer ball.

"Don't touch that!" she whispers sharply. Then she smiles uncomfortably. "We don't want it to get lost or anything, do we dear?" She avoids my eyes and quickly herds him into the van.

My four-year-old tumbles up to my friend and hands her a pink wad of chewed-up bubble gum. "Can you throw that away for me?" she asks sweetly, and then scrambles into her car seat.

My best friend looks at me with her eyes wide and her bubble gum-slathered hand frozen in mid-air.

"It's okay. Don't panic," I say, tripping backwards over my son's broken wagon. "I've got hand sanitizer not ten feet from here. Don't move, I'll be right back."

Seventeen pumps and hand scrubbings later we are ready to go. Slipping her sleeve down over her fingers she opens the passenger door. Then she furtively positions her coat so that not one part of her body will be touching the seat of my car. Satisfied, she grins and takes her seat.

Good, I think, getting into the driver's seat and starting the engine. *She's going to be fine.*

Then I hear her choke. I look over to see her red-faced and pointing to a waxy pile of chunky, brown, gooey stuff melted to the dashboard in front of her.

Oops. Forgot about that one. My son left a brown crayon in the hot car last summer. We never did get around to cleaning it up.

"Is that . . . what I think it is?" she asks.

We look at each other. "Maybe we better take separate cars," I say.

She shakes her head. "No, it's worth it, to spend time with you."

I beam. Compromise, sacrifice, and a blatant overlooking of faults: Three principles that bind us together. No wonder we're best friends. I just hope she still feels the same way tonight after she finds out she set her coat on a half-eaten chocolate chip cookie. Good thing forgiveness is another principle of our friendship. That and the invention of stain remover will ensure we're friends forever.

25

oops, i lost the baby

"Aaargh!" my husband yells in frustration as he opens the shower door. "Where is my towel? I just hung it here a minute ago!"

I laugh. It's another one of those rhetorical questions he is always asking, like, "Who put lipstick on the cat?" Or "Why is there a Lego boat floating in my soup?"

There are no answers to these questions, and if there were, I've forgotten them within the last five minutes. It's a curse that has grown worse with each child. I keep forgetting things like brushing my hair before I go grocery shopping or more important things, like where I live.

I am not the only one this has happened to. This forgetting/losing things phenomenon strikes every parent, and the more children you have, the worse it gets. How else do you explain the fact that I have lost 380 pens in the last month? And that is not the worst thing I have done.

First Child: I'm happily shopping at the mall for an hour before I realize that I don't have my car keys. I frantically rush out to see if I dropped them in the parking lot and find that I have locked them in the car, and the car is still running.

Second Child: I get in the car to take my daughter to ballet. I get halfway down my street before I realize I have forgotten both children at home.

Third Child: I forget the names of my children. "Harold, Cecil, Frederick, Arnold, Gerald, Jerome, Jake, John, Michael, Kelly, Francis . . . Aaaargh! I know you live here and one of these times I'm going to remember your name . . . and then you're in real trouble!"

Fourth Child: My son writes a letter to the tooth fairy and puts it under his pillow. "Dear Tooth Fairy, I've put my tooth under the pillow for twenty-three nights in a row, and it's still there. Now I lost another tooth. Please will you come tonight and pick up my teeth and leave me some money?"

Fifth Child: I turn on the water to wash my hands. I run out of the bathroom when I notice one of the kids has stacked three dining room chairs on top of each other in order to reach my secret stash of candy. After a traumatic crash and several band-aids, I decide I'm too tired to make dinner, so I take all the children to McDonald's for a treat. We've been gone for an hour before I remember that I never turned off the water.

In spite of all this, and the fact that we owe the library hundreds of dollars in late fees, I recently discovered I might not be so crazy after all.

One morning I ventured into the room of my son, the pack rat. I was shocked to find several piles of junk, some looking taller than Mount Everest. I couldn't find the bed or my son. Upon closer inspection I realized that one of the piles was completely made up of black pens.

Me: "Son! We must clean out your room today!"

Son: "What do you mean? I just cleaned it."

Me: "You just cleaned it? Then why is there garbage all over the floor?"

Son: "That's not garbage! Those are my second grade spelling tests."

Me: "And they are on your floor because . . ."

Son: "I might forget how to spell those words someday. Hey, what are you doing? Don't throw that away!"

Me: "It's a moldy sandwich."

Son: "I know, but my best friend traded it to me for my cookie at lunch, and it reminds me of him."

Sifting though the piles, I find things like his collection of old teeth and a pile of dirt from our trip to Yellowstone.

Finally, after several attempts to put items in the garbage, I convince him to let me throw away an old shoe. Not without a fight, however. He had been using it to hold the pile of dirt.

I would be frustrated except I've learned to deal with it from living with his father who has a collection of 233 mugs. After clearing a path to the bed, I decide to give up. Oh, well. At least I found my black pens. Now, where did I put the baby?

26

the dog days of summer

Last summer, my children approached me with lemonade, homemade cookies, and a carefully crafted business proposal explaining how they could achieve the American dream. Basically, it sounded something like this: we get a dog, and you do all the work.

After I finished choking on my lemonade, I explained to them that no dog would cross the threshold of our home as long as there was breath in my body. I tried to ignore the glint I saw in my son's eye.

It's not that I don't trust my children with animals. Okay, it *is* that I don't trust my children with animals. Especially a certain son who likes to stuff cats in drawers and play a game called "Fish Tank Space Invaders," where he bombs the fish with various sinkable items such as dinner forks, dessert plates, and leftover Christmas fruitcake.

My husband doesn't like dogs. He and I have agreed

many times that bringing an animal into our home would be dangerous—for the animal. That's why when he came home from work, puffed out his chest, and announced, "Darlin', we need a huntin' dog," I fainted.

It's not that I don't like dogs. I grew up with a French poodle named, Aber Crombie Terwiliger, nicknamed, "the pirate," because if he didn't like you he would mark you with the "black spot," by going to the bathroom in your bed while you were asleep. Once you received the dreaded spot, you were doomed to receive the same treatment every night, as long as you were sleeping under his skull and crossbones.

Such fond memories may lead you to wonder why I don't want a dog in my own home. The answer is simple. Though the advantages of dogs are many, there is one disadvantage I can't ignore: dogs have bad breath. It's true. Call me squeamish, but I just don't like to breathe in slobbery bad breath if I don't have to. So that is why, when I recovered myself from the shock of my husband's announcement, I put my foot down, saying, "Absolutely no dogs."

"But, honey," said my husband, "I already told my buddy that we'd keep his golden retriever for a week while they went on vacation."

There was a deafening roar as my children all jumped up and chanted, "We're getting a do-og!" and "Maggie" arrived the next day.

The day went something like this:

9:00 AM: Maggie arrives and chews up all the children's toys that look remotely spherical in shape and could be considered a ball.

10:00 AM: Maggie digs leftover chicken bones out of the garbage and deposits them all over the house.

10:15 AM: Maggie throws up on the carpet from eating old chicken bones.

10:30 AM: Baby eats Maggie's dog food.

11:30 AM: Maggie gets mad about being left alone in the house and chews up baby's messy diapers, leaving shreds of diaper everywhere.

1:00 PM: Maggie tries to eat the kitty litter.

2:00 PM: Maggie wakes up my two-year old from her nap because she wants to play ball.

3:00 PM: My daughter comes home from school crying because the kids were mean to her at school. The doorbell rings. It's the neighbor lady, holding Maggie by the collar. "It took us awhile to get her to come out of our house," she says sweetly, "but I finally tempted her with some leftover chicken bones."

Later, my husband, who has fits over spilled milk, said, "Aw, it wasn't that hard to clean up the diapers was it?"

I realized then that aliens had taken over my husband's body.

That night, I peeked into my daughter's room,

feeling guilty that we hadn't talked about her problem at school. Maggie lay curled up next to her on the bed, and my daughter's arm was thrown across her new best friend. I tried not to smell Maggie's breath as I kissed my daughter's cheek. Hmm . . . Perhaps a loyal friend for my daughter was worth a little dog halitosis. I marched back to the bedroom and told my husband that we might be able to get a dog after all—as soon as the baby outgrew his taste for dog food.

27

the roly-poly wars

Last week, my son and I snaked through the jungle that is our backyard, stalking our prey. We were on a dangerous mission of serious consequence. Our failure could result in the loss of hundreds of lives. We were desperate to destroy the enemy at all costs, in order to save those innocent victims: my garden tomatoes. Our weapon? One highly potent bottle of bug spray.

I chose to use the most powerful bug spray money can buy because:

1. I am engaged in a battle to the death with the slugs and crawly things that are trying to devour my garden vegetables.
2. I hate the sound that squishing a bug makes.

When I squish a bug, I have to wear rubber gloves and noise-cancelling earphones. When swatting flies, I prefer the large wimpy distance of a fly-swatter, duct-taped to the end of a tall feather duster. This is an ingenious contraption! It kills bugs with one end (keeping you as far as possible from the ugly deed) and sweeps cobwebs away with the other.

I invented it one day when I noticed a population explosion of roly-polies and spiders in my daughter's basement bedroom. My daughter is an environmentalist. When she was assigned a talk on loving others in primary she wrote a treatise called, "Whales Are People Too and We Should Love Them and Not Pollute Their Homes."

She took one look at my bug-killing contraption and stood in my path, blocking my entrance to her sanctuary.

"What are you doing with that thing?" she asked.

"I'm going to get rid of the spiders in your room," I said, thinking she'd be grateful to me for saving her from vicious crawly creatures of the night.

She glared at me. "That's murder. You can't kill bugs just because you don't like the way they look. They have rights too. How would you like it if somebody squished you because you were ugly?"

I had never thought about it that way. Ignoring her comment on my looks, I asked her, "Well, what do you do with all the bugs when you find them?"

She looked smug and said, "I put them under my pillow because then they can crawl back under my bed where they like it. It's dark under there, and I think they like to eat the crumbs I drop on the floor."

Speechless, I retreated. Later, while she was at a friend's house, I sneaked in with my bug-squishing feather duster and swept away some of the cobwebs. The whole time I imagined getting hate mail from her and her leftist friends.

This is why I was being so secretive about my plan for bug genocide in the backyard garden. I could only imagine what she would say about my destroying an entire mini-ecosystem just to save my peppers and beets.

My son handed me our weapon of choice, a mixture of chemicals so powerful that one spray would destroy generations of roly-polies, slugs, and all creeping things that might set foot, or should I say feet, in our garden.

I read the label. It said, "Don't even think about letting these chemicals touch your skin, or spraying without a mask, helmet, and full body armor. If inhaled, check to see if the person is dead, then call an ambulance and pray."

I looked around, nervously expecting to see my daughter, chained to a cornstalk, wearing a sandwich board that had the words "Slug-Slayer!" printed in red letters, surrounded by pictures of dead roly-polies.

The image was too much. I set down the bottle of bug spray and walked over to a spinach plant.

My son asked, "What's the matter, Mom?"

I looked around at our plethora of produce and said to my son, "Well, when the Good Lord said to share our blessings with others, I guess he could have meant beetles and roly-polies too."

Ignoring the confused stare of my son, I bent over and lifted up a spinach leaf to reveal a fat little slug, happily munching away.

I leaned over and whispered to the slug, "It's okay, little buddy. Go ahead and enjoy. Next year, I'll plant enough for both of us."

28

morning bells are ringing

I hate alarm clocks. They are so annoying. Each morning they are not only loud and obnoxious—two things a mother can't stand—but they also commit the most heinous of all crimes I can possibly think of: they wake me up.

That is why, when my father suggested the craziest solution I had ever heard of one day, I knew it was for me.

"I never use alarm clocks," he said, in his gruff, superior voice when I told him my problem.

My ears perked up. What was this? A solution to the lifelong bane of my existence? My heart began to beat faster.

"Yup. When I was a boy, we didn't have alarm clocks. We had to live by our wits. For fifty years, I've just gone to bed, thinking about what time I want to wake up, and I wake up on time every morning. It works every time.

The system has never failed me."

Hmm. I love creative solutions to problems, the quirkier, the better. But this nutty idea would never work.

I decided to try it. That night, my husband came home late from a meeting to find me in my bed, just ready to implement my plan.

"Honey," he said, in his 'what in heaven's name is going on around here' voice. "Why are the kids out making each other gourmet meals in the kitchen while you are in here sleeping?"

"Huh?" I replied.

"The kids!" he yelled. "They are making doughnuts in the kitchen."

"Speak louder," I requested, cocking my head. "You're mumbling."

He marched over to the bed and yanked the huge bulbous earphones I had saved from the 1970s off of my head.

"I am not mumbling," he said, in a quiet voice. He was practicing his stress-control techniques again. I could tell.

He spoke slowly. "May I ask why I have come home to find you dressed as a space alien in my bed? And what are the kids doing in the kitchen at this hour?"

"Oh, that." I replied, snatching my earphones back and putting them back on my ears. "I wasn't able to hear them with these earphones on. I needed quiet. I'm trying to meditate."

He looked at me for a long time. Then he leaned over and lifted one earphone and whispered, "Meditate? What are you meditating on, precisely?"

I smiled at him. "I'm going to wake up at 5 AM tomorrow. I've got a lot to do."

My husband straightened himself and eyed me while he removed his tie. Then he went to set his alarm clock.

"What in the . . . " he sputtered, "Where is my alarm clock?"

"It's out in the garden," I replied, staring intensely at the poster that I had made and taped to my dresser, which said, "FIVE 'O CLOCK OR BUST."

My husband stumbled out of the bathroom. "Out in the garden?"

"Yup," I said, yelling so that I could hear myself in spite of the earphones. "I threw it out the window."

He stared at me. "Why in the world would you—"

I held up my hand to stop him. "We don't need it any more. I've got this new, kinder, gentler way to wake up. You should be glad," I said, looking into his bulging eyes and pursed lips. "The nasty alarm won't jolt you unceremoniously out of a beautiful sleep every morning with its annoying, jarring noise that hurts your ears."

"I . . . like . . . annoying," he replied. "That is how I wake up. I need to be annoyed. How am I supposed to get to work on time?" He looked slightly panicked.

"I . . . need . . . my . . . alarm . . . clock," he said.

"Please," he added, when he noticed I wasn't moving.

"Don't worry! Honey, just trust me. This idea is going to work. I'll wake you up shortly after I do."

I smiled and patted his hand as he scooted underneath the covers. "Have I ever let you down before?"

He stared at the ceiling. "I think I have a headache," he said, before turning over and covering his head with a pillow. (I needed the light on, so that I could continue to stare at my poster.)

The next morning I awoke naturally and peacefully. I smiled over at my husband, still sleeping soundly with a pillow over his head.

Aaaah. Morning was so beautiful when you could gently ease into it at your own pace. As I padded my way into the bathroom, I discovered the one glitch in my plan. I had thrown my only source for telling time out the window the night before. Oh well. Life would be so much simpler without having to be a slave to the clock anyway.

Wait a minute. Was that the garbage truck? I glanced at myself in the mirror. Uh-oh. The garbage truck always came *after* my husband left for work. I ran towards our bedroom. My husband greeted me in the doorway, staring me down with his bloodshot eyes.

"Your plan didn't work," he croaked. "I'm late."

I smiled and called after him as he madly rushed to find his clothes, "But, honey, didn't you enjoy the peaceful wakening this morning?"

"Peaceful . . . right," he said, running out the door after grabbing a hard piece of sugar-encrusted bread with a hole in the middle for breakfast. The kids had left the bag open when they were making "bread doughnuts" the night before.

Husbands. They just don't appreciate the pure inventiveness it takes to be a wife and mother. Well, back to the drawing board . . . or should I say, poster. Maybe tonight, I would try neon green numbers. They might sink into my subconscious better. I wonder if my husband would mind chanting?

My husband. What would he do without me? He might wake up on time, but what fun is that? He would never have been able to try "bread doughnuts." Now that makes life an adventure worth living, don't you think?

29

sew what?

Sewing. I have often imagined the Lord chuckling to himself as he imagined me trying to master this womanly art. Perhaps He was trying to teach me something when it was decreed in heaven that all square corners must meet together and match perfectly. Humility . . . maybe . . . because for the whimsical, creative, non-analytical mind, square corners are an anomaly . . . an unattainable Nirvana that will continue to taunt us until we die.

Once, as an enthusiastic newly married bride I tried to sew some shorts for my husband.

"Honey, look!" I cried as he wearily trudged through the door after work.

His right eyebrow lifted. "What are those?"

"What do you mean?" I asked, hurt. "They're shorts! So you can play basketball with the guys. Which ones do you like best?"

He stood still, eyeing the red plaid versus the purple paisley. Clearing his throat he admitted cautiously that they were both nice.

"Try them on!" I said impatiently. "I made a few mistakes, but I kind of fixed them as I went on."

He held up the shorts with one hand and a pained look.

"I got the fabric on clearance!" I declared proudly.

"Hmm. I guessed that," he replied.

"What's that supposed to mean?

"Nothing. I'll try them on right now."

Two minutes later he emerged, unsmiling, from the bedroom wearing a pair of purple pantaloons that ballooned out from his waist and sagged below his knees. You could have fit two more of him inside the flapping waistband.

I frowned. "You're not going to wear those to play basketball with the guys, are you?"

"Uhh, no," he grunted.

At least he was honest. But my husband has not been my toughest sewing critic. I didn't meet that person until my oldest son turned eight and joined Cub Scouts.

"Mom! I need these eight patches sewn on by tonight's pack meeting. They're having a uniform inspection!"

"A uniform inspection," I said. "What is this? The army or something?"

My son's eyes grew big. "Worse," he replied. "If I don't pass, they won't give me a cookie at the end of the night."

"Hmmm," I grumbled, retrieving my needle and thread. I began to place the patches around my son's uniform. My son stood over me, shouting out directions and watching me like a hawk.

"Mom, that doesn't go there. You better do a good job or you won't look good tonight."

"Ouch!" I yelled as I stabbed my finger. "What do they make these patches out of? Reinforced rubber? I can hardly push the needle through."

My son sized me up with a long look. "Are you sure you know what you're doing?"

"Of course I know what I'm doing. Now scram. You're making me nervous."

"Okay," he said, running off and returning every five minutes to inspect my work. Finally, I was done.

"It took you long enough," said my son as he peered at the shirt spread out on my lap. He pointed out that several patches were crooked.

Glaring, I tried to yank the shirt off of my lap and hand it to him. Only it wouldn't come off of my lap. I had sewn the patches and the shirt to my pants.

"Aaaaargh!" I yelled.

My son backed away slowly. "I think I'll just come back later," he said as he shot away down the hall.

As I watched his retreating form, my creative, non-analytical brain came up with my next invention: Cub Scout shirts made out of Velcro. Yes! I was going to make a mint off of all the down-trodden, patch slaving, Cub Scout mothers of the world. A light bulb went on in my mind, and an evil smile spread across my face. Then maybe I could afford to buy the material for my next sewing project: a pair of shorts for my son.

30

older but dimmer

It's a proven fact that once a child turns thirteen years old, a parent's IQ score suddenly drops ten points. It's true . . . just ask them. They'll tell you. I found this out the other night while picking up my thirteen-year-old from a church activity.

"Hey, Mom," she exclaimed as she slid into the car, waving at her friends. "We had the most fun *ever!*"

"Really?" I answered. "What did you do? Bake cookies? That was always my favorite thing when I was your age!"

My daughter snorted. "Ah, nooooo . . . That's for the *older* generation mom. We *are* in the twenty-first century you know." She shook her head and tousled her little brother's hair as she buckled herself into her seat.

"Well, it's not like I used to ride in a horse and buggy." I laughed. "My teenage friends and I came up with some pretty brilliant things to do, if I do say so myself."

"Oh yeah? Like what?" she asked, her tone disbelieving.

My younger son piped up. "I believe you, Mom! You're smart. You always help me get my math problems right."

"Thank you, son. I'm glad someone appreciates—"

"Well," he said, and wrinkled his nose in thought, "a little bit smart."

I coughed. "What do you mean, a little bit smart?"

He blushed. "Last night when I asked you what 63 x 89 was, I checked your answer on my calculator and you were wrong."

"You had a calculator in your room?" I asked, incredulous. "Why did you make me do all that work in my head?"

"Because," he replied with a wise air, "my teacher says you have to learn how to do things the old-fashioned way and not rely on technology to do it for you."

"Grrr . . ." I said.

"Exactly my point," said my daughter knowingly from the back seat. "Mom knows about old-fashioned things, but she does not understand the finer complexities of teenagers today."

"Hah!" I cried. "When I was young. We knew how to have fun! We would go downtown with cameras and take hilarious pictures of each other doing crazy stunts on city landmarks."

"Hey," said my son. "I thought you said we should never do crazy things when our friends tell us to."

"Er . . . I didn't mean crazy per se . . . more like . . . interesting poses."

My son's eyes narrowed, "What do you mean by interesting?"

"This," declared my daughter loudly, "is all very fascinating, but it is beside the point. Film cameras are old technology. My friends and I take pictures of each other all the time and edit our snapshots on the computer. It's old news. But I bet you never had as much fun as I did tonight!"

I laughed and raised my hand off of the steering wheel in surrender. "Okay, okay. I admit it. I'll never understand the finer complexities of today. What did you do tonight that was so fun?"

She snickered.

"What? What did you do?"

She smiled and said smugly, "Rubber band fight."

"*Awesome!*" breathed my son.

"You had a rubber band fight?" I asked.

My daughter giggled. "Yeah. We really know how to get creative. I bet you never thought of using rubber bands as ammunition."

"Er, actually . . ." I stuttered.

"Cameras may have been fun in the nineties," she interrupted, "but rubber bands are all the rage in this day and age." She leaned back in her seat with her arms folded. "I bet you can't top that with anything you did when you were young."

I opened my mouth and then closed it. She was right. There was nothing left to say. Rubber bands. The technology of today. Who knew?

I wondered what was up for next week? Water chestnut eating contests? Now that sounded like fun. Remind me to bring my camera.

31

recycle mania

Every once in awhile, I am overcome by an irrepressible urge to be Supermom. The only thing stopping me is that I can't afford the outfit. That is why, when I found out I could save the earth *and* save money by recycling, I went a little off the deep end for a month or two.

"Honey!" I yelled, as I heard my husband trudge through the door after a hard day of work, "Did you know that America throws away enough paper each year to build a twelve foot high wall of paper from coast to coast?"

My husband stared at me for a moment. Then he said, "Did *you* know, that I had to scale a twelve-foot wall of corrugated cardboard in our garage just to make it inside this door?" He muttered something softly to himself as he moved toward the coat closet.

I shrugged. "Sometimes you have to make a few sacrifices in order to save our precious resour—" I had to stop mid-lecture for a deafening crash, when the garbage bag full of aluminum cans I had nailed to the inside of the closet door broke and spilled, leaving my husband buried in aluminum up to his knees.

"You know," I said, unable to suppress my enthusiasm. "Just one of those cans will power a television for three hours!"

My husband stood as though carved in stone, blinking at me.

I edged toward him cautiously. "Why don't I just clean that up for you. You can help me set the table. Can you grab the syrup? We're having pancakes for dinner."

With a stoic look he slogged through the cans toward the refrigerator while I started to clean up. After awhile he said, "Where in heaven's name is the syrup? I've been searching for an eternity."

"In the mustard bottle," I yelled over the noise of the cans dropping in the bag.

My husband straightened up. "The mustard bottle?"

I smiled proudly. "Yeah, I made my own syrup in order to save packaging. Did you know they won't take number four plastic at the recycling center? I thought the mustard bottle was the perfect idea. You can squeeze it out."

My husband's unibrow moved up and down like a caterpillar as if he couldn't figure something out. "Well, where did you put the mustard then?"

I laughed. "In the sour cream container, of course."

"And the sour cream?" he wheezed.

"In the ketchup bottle."

My husband rubbed his forehead. "I think I'll just read the paper 'til dinner. I'm getting a headache."

By dinner time he was feeling much better . . . until he went to reach for his fork.

"Where's my fork?" he asked.

"You don't need a fork, Daddy," said my eight-year-old daughter. "I invented a sort of chopstick spoon out of the styrofoam clamshells from last night's Chinese take-out. Mom says reusing things is even better than recycling."

I beamed.

My daughter continued, "You use it like this, see?" She snapped the mouth of the clamshell open and shut in his face, making his head swivel toward the window to avoid his nose being chopped off.

Then he froze. "What, may I ask, is a four foot pile of eggshells doing in our back yard?"

I patted his hand. "Don't worry. It's just going to be there until the compost bin I ordered arrives."

He stared at me. "How much was that?"

"It's okay," I replied with excitement. "I did the calculations, and it'll pay for itself in twenty-eight years."

My husband stood up. "I think I need to lie down."

I ran after him, "Wait, um . . . before you lie down I should warn you, the kids and I were working on a little project . . ."

My husband's jaw dropped when he saw the gigantic cottage cheese container igloo that took up the whole king-sized bed.

"It's a dog igloo, you know, like the ones they sell at the store. Only ours was free!"

"But . . . we . . . don't . . . have . . . a . . . dog," said my husband.

"I know that," I said, rolling my eyes. "But *someone* does. I'm sure somebody can use it."

That's when my husband fainted. No just kidding, but when his hand reached up to clutch his chest, I decided that I'd better tone down the recycling crusade in order to protect the health of his heart.

It's okay. He'll feel better tomorrow when I make him his favorite dinner—steak and homemade fries. Now, if only I can remember where I put the ketchup.

32

how to prepare for a talk

Every time the bishop asks me to give a talk I say things like, "Thank you! I've always wished someone would ask me to give a talk on symbolism and ecology in the book of Revelations!"

But what I'm really thinking is, "I wonder how many downward facing dog poses it will take me to lose five pounds in five days."

Then I hang up the phone and rush to prepare. There's no time to lose. I dash to the bathroom mirror to inspect the packaging. Holy crow's feet! My eyes widen in horror as I realize I have turned one hundred years old overnight!

Grimly, I lean forward and inspect the puffy bags beneath my eyes. Oh, that's bad. I try to suck them back into my eyeballs with a fearful stare. No luck. That just dries out my eyeballs and turns them into a zombie shade of spidery red. I shake my head back and forth to loosen my dried up eyelids and notice some jiggling skin by my neck. Jowls! I have jowls! When did that happen? Soberly, I gather up the loose skin on either side of my face and stuff it back into the sides of my mouth, trying to hold it between my teeth. I lift one eyebrow. Hey, that's not bad.

"Mommy, what are you doing?"

I look down at my four-year-old, and she jumps, startled by my spidery eyeballs and cadaverous cheeks. As soon as I open my mouth to talk, the traitorous jowls slither out of their holding cell and wiggle merrily like bowls of gelatin attached to either side of my face.

Sighing, I rush downstairs and burrow through my vast collection of exercise videos, as numerous as the sands of the sea, which have been collecting dust on my bookshelves since the day after I tried each one of them.

Which one will give me the fastest results? Aha! I run to the video player and slide in *Burn and Churn Fat Annihilator: Three Hours to a New You.*

"And kick and jump and twist and turn—" The lively music attracts my kids like flypaper to my legs.

"I want to try . . . let me try, Mommy!" My two-year-old has suction cupped his arms and legs to my knee and my four-year-old is trying to scale up my backside. I am finding it harder and harder to do jumping jacks.

"Do it again, Mommy!" squeals my son as I try to Frankenstein march in spite of his koala-bear grip on my leg. Ouch. I think I strained a muscle. Maybe I should have stuck with the downward facing dog idea. Slowly, I ease my body down into the familiar yoga pose. It's the only yoga pose I remember how to do since I lost my yoga DVD to a kid game of indoor Ultimate Frisbee.

"A slide, a slide!" yells my daughter.

I try to maintain my dignified downward facing dog sereneness as my two youngest children climb up my legs and slide down my back. It's mighty hard to get the right "ohm" sound when people are landing on your head, I can tell you that.

The good news is I can feel my jowls rolling up over my cheeks and my puffy bags seeping back into my eyelids where they belong. I wonder if the bishop would let me give my talk upside-down. I think I could work it into the symbolism idea. Last year he didn't even flinch when Rhonda Wilkins juggled powdered milk boxes as an object lesson in her talk on food storage.

Yes! I feel ten years younger already. Now I wonder where I put that year's supply of cellulite eraser cream? The lady who sold it to me before last year's church talk said I would see results in three days. Anything has got to be better than this, *ouch,* yoga slide. That's it. I'm going to take a strong aspirin and meditate on the symbolism I can find while reading the scriptures upside down. It's going to be my best talk ever!

33

sunbeam sundae

I believe in object lessons, especially ones that involve food. The only lesson I can remember from my kindergarten years involved a balloon, a hard boiled egg, and an old fluorescent light tube. The teacher performed such an amazing feat with these three objects that to this day I still remember it . . . not the feat, or the lesson, but I remember the objects. And that is why object lessons are so important. You never forget them.

This is why, when I was asked to teach a sunbeam class, I knew I had to come up with the greatest object lesson ever known to mankind. It had to be something the kids would never forget. Aspiring to the greatness of the hard-boiled egg wielding teacher of my youth, I wracked my brain to come up with a brilliant plan. The lesson was on forgiveness. Think. Think. Think. What was the *one* item that popped into every person's head when they thought about forgiveness? Of course! A giant chocolate fudge sundae! And so a legendary object lesson was born.

"Now, class," I said to the six cherubic four-year-olds all lined up in a row. "Who likes ice cream?"

Immediately, six dimpled hands shot up in the air, even the one that had been in little Jimmy's nose.

"Okay, I thought so. Today we are going to learn that it is important to forgive one another. Who knows what forgiveness means?"

Austin raised his hand. "I got a new red truck yesterday." Then he reached over and poked Jane, the girl sitting next to him, in the arm.

"That's nice," I replied, calling on Emma next. "Do you know what forgiveness means?"

Emma looked thoughtful for a moment, and she then pulled the bottom of her green velvet dress up over her head.

Austin said, "Sometimes my daddy [poke] says bad words [poke, poke] when he's driving the car [poke, poke, poke]."

I cleared my throat loudly.

Jane, the beautiful child who was getting poked to death, raised her good arm. She looked sweetly at me with her large blue eyes and said, "I don't like you. I want my old teacher back."

I stood up. This was going nowhere. Time to break

out my brilliant object lesson. "Okay, kids, now I am going to make you a delicious ice cream sundae! What do you think of that?"

Cheers erupted from six little cupid lips. Well, all except for Jane who was folding her arms and looking as if she had just eaten a lemon. Austin yelled into Jane's ear, "Hey, [poke] we're getting ice cream [poke, poke]." Then he grinned up at me and poked her in the leg for good measure.

"All right, now ," I said, clapping my hands for quiet. "This vanilla ice cream is like the happy feelings you get when you play with your friends."

Emma said, "I only like chocolate ice cream."

"Well, in any case," I replied, "Either chocolate *or* vanilla ice cream is your happy feelings. Now when your friend shares with you, you feel even happier. Austin, stop poking Jane, and come up here. Tell me your favorite topping."

Austin crawled underneath his chair and said, "I don't like nuts."

I sighed. "Okay . . . what do you like? Chocolate fudge?"

He nodded and crawled closer as I explained that chocolate fudge is how happy we feel when we are sharing and being nice.

"Now class, what kinds of feelings do the ice cream represent?"

"Oh, oh, I know!" shouted Emma. "Chocolate feelings."

I stared at her. "No. The ice cream is happy feelings. Happy feelings. Does everybody understand?"

Jimmy nodded wisely while sucking his thumb. Jane glared at me.

"So now I'm going to show how Austin feels when his friend is mean to him." I took out a Ziploc bag full of dirt. Twelve little eyes got big and round. "Who would like to pour this dirt all over the chocolate sundae that Austin made?"

I saw a slow smile creep across Jane's face. She raised her hand. Still smiling, she marched up, took the bag of dirt and dumped it on top of the ice cream. Then she poked Austin in the arm and sat down.

A great weeping and wailing and gnashing of teeth that could be heard throughout the church building rose up within the walls of the classroom.

"No, no. Stop crying," I said, running from child to child. "Please, I haven't got to the point yet . . . we're going to forgive the friend and eat ice cream together!"

In the midst of the chaos, I felt someone yanking on the bottom of my sweater. I turned around to see Jane, her bright eyes smiling up at me. "Teacher, I like you," she said, reaching up to take my hand.

Well, like I said. It was one brilliant object lesson that they weren't likely to forget. And it taught the children one important lesson: the more you cry in Sunbeam class, the more ice cream your teacher will pile in your bowl to keep you quiet. And that's why you should always teach with an object lesson. Pass the maraschinos!

34

desperate measures

It's four o'clock in the morning. I steal through the blackened rooms of my house, feeling my way toward the kitchen. I am a thief in the night, trying to steal that most elusive family jewel: time to myself.

I try not to scream as I stub my toe on that cursed Tonka truck that seems to trip me every time I need to go somewhere fast. I hop on one foot, practicing the Lamaze breathing techniques that are so familiar to me after birthing five children.

I should have known this would happen. There are always consequences when any parent tries to sneak some alone time. Like the time I asked my ten-year-old to watch the baby while I took a shower. I came out five minutes later to find the baby crouching on top of the table, smiling, with one hand buried elbow deep in the honey container. Honey had been smeared all over the table and all over every part of his chubby little body. My ten-year-old was watching television.

Some people will take extraordinary measures to get their alone time, but that can be dangerous. I know of a lady who tried to go to the bathroom without an audience of four children. She locked the door and sighed, saying, "I'll just be a minute," to the little fists pounding on the door. Finally there was silence. She breathed deeply, enjoying every moment of peace until she saw a butcher knife sliding underneath the bathroom door, accompanied by a little voice saying, "Don't worry Mommy! I'll cut you out of there!"

The more desperate parents become, the more creative they get, but creative alone time can be humiliating. A friend called me the other day from the produce section of the grocery store.

"This is great!" she gushed. "It's the first time I've had to myself in a couple of weeks!"

I decided to try it, even though my husband was skeptical. "Sure, I'll watch the kids while you go grocery shopping," he said, "but why do you need to take a romance novel to the supermarket?"

Rats! What was I supposed to say to that? I smiled and started to back out the door. "Oh, you know those long check-out lines," I said, waving and blowing kisses to all the little noses and hands pressed against the living room window.

Once I got to the store, I bought myself three

doughnuts, reveling in the fact that I didn't have to share with any sticky little fingers. I brought the doughnuts out to my car and sat in the driver's seat, wickedly eating doughnuts and devouring my romance novel.

I was just getting to the good part when I saw a friend waving and starting toward me from her car in the parking lot. Oh no! My only thought before I left had been to escape. I had no make-up on and I was still wearing my Daffy Duck flannel pajama bottoms. Reluctantly, I rolled down the window.

"What are you reading?" she asked, peering into the car. Then she pointed. "Are all those doughnuts for you?"

Like I said, trying to get time to yourself while the world is still awake can be humiliating.

I sit down to nurse my injury and am surprised to realize that I miss all those cute little pink lips, vying to be the first to kiss my "owie" all better. I look around. The house is too quiet. I miss the commotion. Will this deafening silence fill my house every day after all my little ones have grown and gone?

I shiver and steal back to my bed, climbing over the two children who have slithered in and snuggled next to my husband. There are four people and a cat in my bed. It's crowded, but I smile as I softly stroke my son's dimpled cheek, thinking, "There'll be time enough to be alone in the years to come."

Laughter Is the Best Medicine

Read additional humorous essays on the family
by Kersten Campbell and share your own funny
stories at www.kerstencampbell.com.